Contents

Fish Illustrations: Trevor Hawkins

Published in 2025 by
Australian Fishing Network Pty Ltd
PO Box 544, Croydon, VIC 3136
Tel: (03) 9729 8788 Email: sales@afn.com.au www.afn.com.au

 ISBN 9781 8651 3437 6

DISCLAIMER

The solar/lunar bite times in this book were derived from the program* WXTide32 *and are predictions. While they are as accurate as possible, they should be used as a guide only. Local conditions and changes can cause variations, so consult a website such as the* Bureau of Meteorology Oceanographic Services, (www.bom.gov.au/oceanography/tides) *as close as possible to the tide date and time before your fishing trip for the most up-to-date information and if you require certified information.
The publisher, Australian Fishing Network, advises that the information in this guide should not be used for navigation and should not be relied on for crucial situations.

"This product is based on Bureau of Meteorology information that has subsequently been modified. The Bureau does not necessarily support or endorse, or have any connection with, the product.
In respect of that part of the information which is sourced from the Bureau, and to the maximum extent permitted by law:
(i) The Bureau makes no representation and gives no warranty of any kind whether express, implied, statutory or otherwise in respect to the availability, accuracy, currency, completeness, quality or reliability of the information or that the information will be fit for any particular purpose or will not infringe any third party Intellectual Property rights; and
(ii) the Bureau's liability for any loss, damage, cost or expense resulting from use of, or reliance on, the information is entirely excluded."
"The Bureau of Meteorology gives no warranty of any kind whether express, implied, statutory or otherwise in respect to the availability, accuracy, currency, completeness, quality or reliability of the information or that the information will be fit for any particular purpose or will not infringe any third party Intellectual Property rights. The Bureau's liability for any loss, damage, cost or expense resulting from use of, or reliance on, the information is entirely excluded."

'Solunar' theory suggests all creatures great and small respond in some way to the influences of both the Sun and the Moon during the course of a day.

This book lists the peak activity times along with the moon phases and it should become an indispensable tool for when you're planning a trip.
The peak activity times are presented in this book to simulate the logical progression of the Moon as it orbits the Earth. The first is the minor peak at moonrise, no matter what time of day at which it occurs. The second the major peak when the moon is directly overhead, the third is the minor peak at moonset and the fourth is the major peak when the moon is directly overhead on the opposite side of the globe.

Solunar (solar and lunar) theory is one of nature's mysteries which many of us find difficult to consider with any merit. A number of books, tables and articles have been written on the subject of lunar and solar influences on animal behaviour. Solunar theory suggests all creatures great and small respond in some way to the influences of both the Sun and the Moon during the course of a day. Specifically this response is often seen as an increase or decrease in activity level. Increased activity periods have often been referred to as peak or prime times.
The combination of centrifugal force produced by the Earth's rotation and the Moon's daily crossing of the sky generates our tides. Such enormous force is produced by these phenomena that it causes the Earth's surface to bulge up to 16 centimetres. Could lunar cycles impact on man? You be the judge. The human gestation period is 266 days, the average synodic interval between two consecutive new Moons is 29.530589 days; 266 divided by 29.530589 equals 9.008 lunar months. Sound familiar? Man is made up of approximately 80 per cent water. We know what happens tidally to huge bodies of water. Do you think there is a remote possibility that we too could unknowingly experience the effects of this heavenly sphere?

It is important to understand that what influences one creature may not influence another in any circumstance. For example there are a number of intertidal organisms that are most active when submerged by an incoming tide, creatures such as barnacles, green crabs, snails, clams, and oysters. Others, like soldier crabs and shorebirds, are especially adapted to feed on beaches exposed at low tide. The lower the creature's order in the animal kingdom the more likely it is to respond to solar and lunar stimuli.

LIGHT THEORY

The light theory suggests that light levels during the day and night dictate feeding activity times. For example it is said that fishing is better on the mornings immediately leading up to and following the period of new Moon because the fish have been unable to feed during the periods of low light during the night. Fishing is also said to be good during the nights leading up to and following the full Moon because of increased evening light levels.

SOLAR THEORY

To some extent the solar theory is reliant upon seasonal changes, therefore I have provided you with a brief summary of the seasonal patterns and how they influence the Southern Hemisphere.

he principle of the solar theory works on the various istances of the Sun's rise, upper transit, set, and wer transit to identify the peak activity periods. ollowing a long period of darkness the animal ingdom is given a kick-start to the day as dawn pproaches. Many creatures stir from their rest period nd warm with the Sun to commence the daily routine f food gathering. All animal life has a preferred emperature range and fish are no exception to this ule. It is said that seasonal conditions may dictate hen particular fish species will commence to feed.

So although dawn and dusk have been historically noted as prime fishing times if we review the seasonal fluctuations in day and night time temperatures we may see cause for reassessing our reliance on these times. For example during the colder months peak feeding times may coincide during the warmest time of the day; just after midday when the water temperatures have increased to a more preferred level. Conversely, during the warmer months peak feeding times may align with the coolest times of the day; dusk 'til dawn.

SEASONS

Point A
Northern Hemisphere during fall. The Sun is high overhead at the equator and rays from the Sun fall equally on both the Southern and Northern Hemispheres.

Point B
Northern Hemisphere during winter. A lesser amount of the Sun's rays fall on the Northern Hemisphere where the Sun is low in the sky.

Point C
Northern Hemisphere during springtime. The Sun is high overhead at the equator and rays from the Sun fall equally on both the Southern and Northern Hemispheres.

Point D
Northern Hemisphere during summertime. A majority of the Sun's rays fall on the Northern Hemisphere where the Sun is high overhead.

A N Fall S
B N Winter S
C N Spring S
D N Summer S

LUNAR THEORY

To help you understand the lunar theory in more depth I have provided a brief outline of the various lunar phases. When you watch the Moon over a course of several days you will see that its appearance changes. The varying appearances called 'phases' depend upon the relative positions of the Sun and Moon.

MOON PHASES

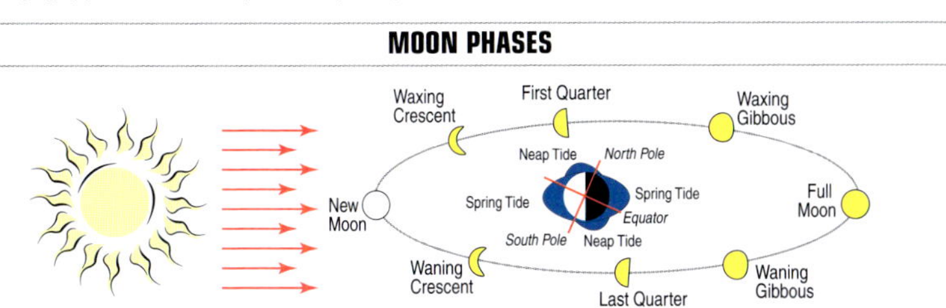

NEW MOON

When the Moon is between the Sun and the Earth we cannot see any of the illuminated side of the Moon, the Moon is dark, we call this phase the new Moon and it is the beginning of a new lunar month. The Moon rises and sets with the Sun during the new Moon. The gravitational forces exerted on the Earth by the Moon and the Sun is greatest at this time. The first of the spring tides for the lunar month occurs during this period.

FIRST QUARTER

The amount of lighted surface visible from the Earth begins to grow and we see a waxing crescent Moon. When the Moon reaches the first quarter we see half of it lit. The Moon rises during the middle of the day and is overhead about dusk and sets around midnight. The Moon's illuminated side will appear on the right in the Northern Hemisphere. The gravitational forces on the Earth have reduced since the new Moon and now the combined pull of the Moon and the Sun is at a minimum for the lunar month. The first of the neap tides for the Lunar month occurs at this time.

FULL MOON

As the illuminated portion grows we have a waxing gibbous Moon. The full Moon occurs when the Moon reaches the side of the Earth opposite from the Sun. It appears large and bright. The Moon rises as the Sun is setting—it is overhead about midnight and sets close to dawn. Th gravitational forces on the Earth have increased sinc the first quarter and now the combined pull of the Moon and the Sun is at a maximum again for the lun month, the second of the spring tides occur.

LAST QUARTER

The gravitational forces on the Earth have reduced since the full Moon and now the combined pull of the Moon and the Sun is at a minimum again for the lunar month. The second of the neap tides for the lunar month occurs at this tim As a waning crescent, the Moon diminishes to a thin sliver, returning to a new Moon after approximately 29.5 solar days or one lunar month. As the Moon revolves around the Earth it rotates on its own axis a the same rate it revolves, therefore the Moon always keeps the same face toward the Earth.

TIDAL FORCES

As the Earth rotates on its axis once every 24 hours relative to the Sun, and 24 hours and 53 minutes relative to the Moon; the Moon rises approximately 53 minutes later with respect to the Sun each day. This delay or lagging can be seen in the variation of tides from day to day.

The principle of the lunar theory works on the various instances of the Moon's rise, upper transit, set, and lower transit to identify the peak activity periods. This theory can also take into account the various lunar phases and the proximity (apogee and perigee) of the Moon to the Earth during the period of one lunation (new Moon to new Moon). Because the Moon orbits the Earth on an elliptical path, the distance between the two is always changing. The Moon has less gravitational influence on the Earth around the time c apogee when the distance between the two bodies is at a maximum. Greater gravitational influence occurs around the time of perigee when the distance betwee the Earth and the Moon is at a minimum.

SOLUNAR THEORY

Solunar theory accounts for the peaks associated wit both the solar and lunar theories. It also incorporates the Sun's lower transit (midnight), and it also flags the coinciding times of peaks from the other theories In other words it takes an each way bet on the three individual theories. Additionally the solunar theory ecognises the gravitational effect on the Earth from he combined force produced by the Moon and the Sun in tandem. This gravitational force changes with he seasons, with the phases of the Moon, and with he Sun and Moon's proximity to Earth.

EFFECTS ON FISHING

ishing wise, catch rates are often said to be higher around the new and full Moon phases. This makes sense when you consider the increased gravitational nfluence on the Earth during these periods. However his is further bolstered if you consider that during hese times we are provided with three windows of peak activity level during general daylight hours, each coinciding with dawn, noon, or dusk. Around he period of new Moon, the Moon is in harmony with he Sun, they rise, transit and set together. During the period of full Moon, the Moon and Sun directly oppose each other, the Moon sets when the Sun rises, the Moon is underfoot at noon, and the Moon rises at Sun set. Whether or not the increased activity levels in lower organisms is the catalyst for larger and perhaps predatory creatures to begin feeding is arguable. Your observations will also show increased activity levels in the non predatory herbivore family during the peak times.

FEEDING PATTERNS

Does activity occur outside of these peak periods? Of course. Remember not all species will react in an identical manner during the peak times. The bottom line is fish don't always feel hungry! They follow certain feeding patterns but aren't totally immune to sampling the odd tid-bit throughout the course of the day. As with most creatures, strength is gained through struggle; and only the fittest and strongest survive in the wild. While minimum work for maximum return is the hallmark of big fish, a fish's condition and health must also be maintained through foraging for food. Natural rhythms aside, fish are also subject to local conditions such as the various fluctuations in air temperature, barometric pressure, water levels, water clarity, and water temperature. These should all be considered when using the tables.

BITE TIME ADJUSTMENTS (Minutes)

Approximate variation times only, taken from various sources.

BITE TIMES

Adelaide	0
Ardrossin	+5
Black Point	+5
Cape Jervis	0
Cape Jervis	0
Ceduna	+20
Clare Bay	+25
Coffin Bay	+10
Coober Pedy	+20
Cook	+30
Fowlers Bay	+25
Kangaroo Island	+5
Kingston SE	-5
Marion Bay	+5
Mt Gambier	-10
Murray Bridge	0
Outer Harbour	0
Port Augusta	+5
Port Gawler	0
Port Lincoln	+10
Port Vincent	+5
Renmark	-10
Robe	-5
Sceale Bay	+20
Smoky Bay	+20
Streaky Bay	+20
Victor Harbour	0
Whyalla	+5
Yorke Peninsula	+5

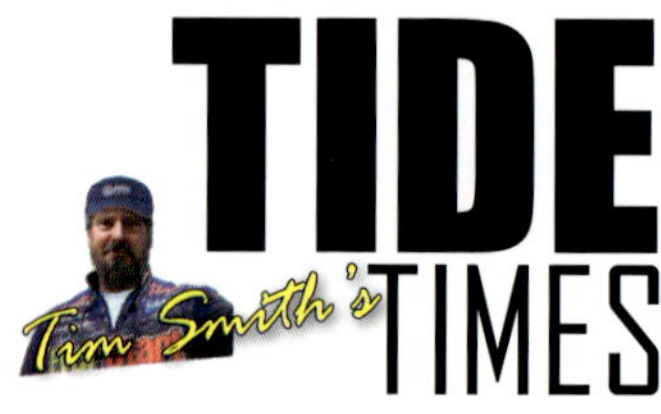

Adelaide Outer Harbour

POPULAR TIDE ADJUSTMENTS

Ardossan	-6min
Brighton	-4min
Cape Jervis	- 30min
Edithburgh	- 30min
Glenelg	-10min
Port Noarlunga	-15min
Port Stanvac	-7min
Port Wakefield	- 10min
Rapid Bay	- 5min
Second Valley	-3min
Port Vincent	- 30min

Day	Date		Tide 1
Mon	1		1:22 AM (0.63) L
Tue	2		1:26 AM (0.80) L
Wed	3		12:38 AM (0.97) L
Thu	4		5:42 AM (1.64) **H**
Fri	5		5:05 AM (1.81) **H**
Sat	6		5:07 AM (1.96) **H**
Sun	7		5:15 AM (2.07) **H**
Mon	8	○	5:23 AM (2.17) **H**
Tue	9		5:34 AM (2.29) **H**
Wed	10		5:50 AM (2.41) **H**
Thu	11		12:00 AM (0.41) L
Fri	12		12:08 AM (0.47) L
Sat	13		12:11 AM (0.49) L
Sun	14		12:14 AM (0.46) L
Mon	15		12:24 AM (0.45) L
Tue	16		12:31 AM (0.53) L
Wed	17		12:16 AM (0.67) L
Thu	18		5:57 AM (1.72) **H**
Fri	19		5:07 AM (1.81) **H**
Sat	20		4:53 AM (1.99) **H**
Sun	21		4:54 AM (2.16) **H**
Mon	22	●	4:59 AM (2.29) **H**
Tue	23		5:07 AM (2.41) **H**
Wed	24		5:21 AM (2.51) **H**
Thu	25		5:41 AM (2.57) **H**
Fri	26		6:02 AM (2.59) **H**
Sat	27		6:22 AM (2.57) **H**
Sun	28		12:09 AM (0.50) L
Mon	29		12:23 AM (0.54) L
Tue	30		12:37 AM (0.62) L

SEPTEMBER 2025

Tide 2		Tide 3		Tide 4	
8:08 AM	(2.32) **H**	2:31 PM	(1.02) L	7:36 PM	(1.65) **H**
8:32 AM	(2.09) **H**	3:12 PM	(1.31) L	6:41 PM	(1.42) **H**
8:41 AM	(1.78) **H**	10:56 PM	(0.86) L		
9:46 AM	(1.42) L	3:41 PM	(2.04) **H**	10:41 PM	(0.59) L
10:06 AM	(1.09) L	4:12 PM	(2.34) **H**	10:54 PM	(0.39) L
10:28 AM	(0.83) L	4:37 PM	(2.53) **H**	11:09 PM	(0.29) L
10:48 AM	(0.64) L	4:58 PM	(2.61) **H**	11:22 PM	(0.28) L
11:08 AM	(0.50) L	5:16 PM	(2.60) **H**	11:35 PM	(0.31) L
11:32 AM	(0.41) L	5:35 PM	(2.52) **H**	11:48 PM	(0.35) L
12:00 PM	(0.39) L	5:56 PM	(2.38) **H**		
6:09 AM	(2.50) **H**	12:28 PM	(0.44) L	6:15 PM	(2.18) **H**
6:28 AM	(2.56) **H**	12:52 PM	(0.55) L	6:28 PM	(1.99) **H**
6:45 AM	(2.58) **H**	1:09 PM	(0.67) L	6:35 PM	(1.85) **H**
7:02 AM	(2.55) **H**	1:21 PM	(0.81) L	6:40 PM	(1.76) **H**
7:19 AM	(2.45) **H**	1:33 PM	(0.98) L	6:36 PM	(1.66) **H**
7:32 AM	(2.23) **H**	1:36 PM	(1.22) L	6:00 PM	(1.58) **H**
7:15 AM	(1.91) **H**	11:26 PM	(0.73) L		
10:42 AM	(1.34) L	4:11 PM	(1.96) **H**	10:49 PM	(0.61) L
10:20 AM	(1.00) L	4:20 PM	(2.22) **H**	10:47 PM	(0.47) L
10:30 AM	(0.71) L	4:35 PM	(2.38) **H**	10:54 PM	(0.39) L
10:44 AM	(0.53) L	4:49 PM	(2.44) **H**	11:01 PM	(0.38) L
10:58 AM	(0.42) L	5:01 PM	(2.43) **H**	11:06 PM	(0.38) L
11:14 AM	(0.36) L	5:14 PM	(2.38) **H**	11:14 PM	(0.38) L
11:34 AM	(0.34) L	5:31 PM	(2.31) **H**	11:27 PM	(0.38) L
11:58 AM	(0.37) L	5:51 PM	(2.22) **H**	11:41 PM	(0.41) L
12:22 PM	(0.44) L	6:09 PM	(2.10) **H**	11:56 PM	(0.46) L
12:43 PM	(0.52) L	6:26 PM	(2.00) **H**		
6:40 AM	(2.53) **H**	1:02 PM	(0.61) L	6:40 PM	(1.90) **H**
6:58 AM	(2.46) **H**	1:22 PM	(0.72) L	6:54 PM	(1.80) **H**
7:18 AM	(2.33) **H**	1:45 PM	(0.89) L	7:04 PM	(1.62) **H**

POPULAR TIDE ADJUSTMENTS

Ardossan	-6min
Brighton	-4min
Cape Jervis	- 30min
Edithburgh	- 30min
Glenelg	-10min
Port Noarlunga	-15min
Port Stanvac	-7min
Port Wakefield	- 10min
Rapid Bay	- 5min
Second Valley	-3min
Port Vincent	- 30min

Adelaide Outer Harbour

Day	Date	Tide 1
Wed	1	12:43 AM (0.77) L
Thu	2	12:03 AM (0.95) L
Fri	3	5:00 AM (1.66) **H**
Sat	4	4:23 AM (1.88) **H**
Sun	5	5:27 AM (2.10) **H**
Mon	6	5:37 AM (2.27) **H**
Tue	7 ○	5:47 AM (2.40) **H**
Wed	8	5:57 AM (2.53) **H**
Thu	9	12:04 AM (0.46) L
Fri	10	12:13 AM (0.50) L
Sat	11	12:19 AM (0.53) L
Sun	12	12:23 AM (0.52) L
Mon	13	12:32 AM (0.49) L
Tue	14	12:47 AM (0.49) L
Wed	15	1:02 AM (0.61) L
Thu	16	12:52 AM (0.82) L
Fri	17	6:04 AM (1.65) **H**
Sat	18	5:04 AM (1.84) **H**
Sun	19	4:58 AM (2.12) **H**
Mon	20	5:08 AM (2.34) **H**
Tue	21 ●	5:21 AM (2.49) **H**
Wed	22	5:35 AM (2.60) **H**
Thu	23	5:52 AM (2.67) **H**
Fri	24	6:13 AM (2.69) **H**
Sat	25	12:12 AM (0.51) L
Sun	26	12:29 AM (0.56) L
Mon	27	12:45 AM (0.60) L
Tue	28	1:01 AM (0.64) L
Wed	29	1:19 AM (0.72) L
Thu	30	1:36 AM (0.89) L
Fri	31	1:13 AM (1.13) L

OCTOBER 2025

Tide 2			Tide 3			Tide 4		
7:37 AM	(2.10)	**H**	2:09 PM	(1.17)	L	6:33 PM	(1.40)	**H**
7:23 AM	(1.77)	**H**	10:19 PM	(0.88)	L			
9:40 AM	(1.32)	L	3:23 PM	(1.92)	**H**	10:02 PM	(0.61)	L
9:49 AM	(0.94)	L	3:50 PM	(2.23)	**H**	10:14 PM	(0.40)	L
11:11 AM	(0.63)	L	5:16 PM	(2.41)	**H**	11:30 PM	(0.33)	L
11:33 AM	(0.42)	L	5:39 PM	(2.44)	**H**	11:44 PM	(0.34)	L
11:56 AM	(0.30)	L	5:58 PM	(2.37)	**H**	11:55 PM	(0.40)	L
12:20 PM	(0.25)	L	6:15 PM	(2.24)	**H**			
6:13 AM	(2.64)	**H**	12:46 PM	(0.27)	L	6:34 PM	(2.07)	**H**
6:33 AM	(2.69)	**H**	1:13 PM	(0.37)	L	6:49 PM	(1.88)	**H**
6:53 AM	(2.68)	**H**	1:34 PM	(0.52)	L	6:59 PM	(1.73)	**H**
7:11 AM	(2.62)	**H**	1:46 PM	(0.67)	L	7:05 PM	(1.66)	**H**
7:27 AM	(2.53)	**H**	1:52 PM	(0.80)	L	7:09 PM	(1.64)	**H**
7:43 AM	(2.37)	**H**	2:01 PM	(0.93)	L	7:12 PM	(1.60)	**H**
7:55 AM	(2.12)	**H**						
7:36 AM	(1.81)	**H**	1:25 PM	(1.33)	L	5:32 PM	(1.53)	**H**
11:06 AM	(1.24)	L	4:40 PM	(1.75)	**H**	10:51 PM	(0.81)	L
10:48 AM	(0.88)	L	4:46 PM	(2.00)	**H**	10:52 PM	(0.62)	L
11:03 AM	(0.59)	L	5:04 PM	(2.17)	**H**	11:04 PM	(0.50)	L
11:21 AM	(0.40)	L	5:22 PM	(2.23)	**H**	11:15 PM	(0.46)	L
11:39 AM	(0.29)	L	5:39 PM	(2.23)	**H**	11:25 PM	(0.45)	L
11:59 AM	(0.25)	L	5:55 PM	(2.19)	**H**	11:38 PM	(0.45)	L
12:20 PM	(0.25)	L	6:14 PM	(2.12)	**H**	11:54 PM	(0.47)	L
12:45 PM	(0.30)	L	6:36 PM	(2.04)	**H**			
6:36 AM	(2.66)	**H**	1:09 PM	(0.37)	L	6:56 PM	(1.94)	**H**
6:58 AM	(2.60)	**H**	1:31 PM	(0.47)	L	7:14 PM	(1.85)	**H**
7:17 AM	(2.53)	**H**	1:51 PM	(0.56)	L	7:30 PM	(1.78)	**H**
7:37 AM	(2.44)	**H**	2:12 PM	(0.66)	L	7:48 PM	(1.70)	**H**
8:02 AM	(2.30)	**H**	2:42 PM	(0.81)	L	8:11 PM	(1.55)	**H**
8:30 AM	(2.06)	**H**	3:31 PM	(1.04)	L	8:36 PM	(1.33)	**H**
9:03 AM	(1.71)	**H**	9:27 PM	(1.04)	L			

POPULAR TIDE ADJUSTMENTS

Ardossan	-6min
Brighton	-4min
Cape Jervis	- 30min
Edithburgh	- 30min
Glenelg	-10min
Port Noarlunga	-15min
Port Stanvac	-7min
Port Wakefield	- 10min
Rapid Bay	- 5min
Second Valley	-3min
Port Vincent	- 30min

Adelaide Outer Harbour

Day	Date		Tide 1
Sat	1		4:38 AM (1.58) **H**
Sun	2		4:17 AM (1.90) **H**
Mon	3		4:32 AM (2.20) **H**
Tue	4		4:51 AM (2.41) **H**
Wed	5		5:09 AM (2.57) **H**
Thu	6	○	5:26 AM (2.69) **H**
Fri	7		5:47 AM (2.76) **H**
Sat	8		6:12 AM (2.76) **H**
Sun	9		6:36 AM (2.69) **H**
Mon	10		12:04 AM (0.64) L
Tue	11		12:22 AM (0.63) L
Wed	12		12:48 AM (0.68) L
Thu	13		1:19 AM (0.83) L
Fri	14		1:50 AM (1.09) L
Sat	15		4:26 AM (1.46) **H**
Sun	16		3:24 AM (1.82) **H**
Mon	17		3:52 AM (2.15) **H**
Tue	18		4:20 AM (2.40) **H**
Wed	19		4:45 AM (2.56) **H**
Thu	20	●	5:09 AM (2.65) **H**
Fri	21		5:33 AM (2.69) **H**
Sat	22		5:59 AM (2.70) **H**
Sun	23		6:25 AM (2.66) **H**
Mon	24		12:23 AM (0.65) L
Tue	25		12:46 AM (0.69) L
Wed	26		1:09 AM (0.74) L
Thu	27		1:38 AM (0.82) L
Fri	28		2:18 AM (0.96) L
Sat	29		3:29 AM (1.17) L
Sun	30		12:44 AM (1.62) **H**

Tide 2		Tide 3		Tide 4	
9:36 AM	(1.29) L	3:17 PM	(1.74) **H**	9:50 PM	(0.77) L
10:10 AM	(0.87) L	4:11 PM	(2.01) **H**	10:17 PM	(0.59) L
10:43 AM	(0.53) L	4:48 PM	(2.15) **H**	10:42 PM	(0.52) L
11:14 AM	(0.31) L	5:18 PM	(2.15) **H**	11:01 PM	(0.55) L
11:43 AM	(0.19) L	5:44 PM	(2.06) **H**	11:16 PM	(0.60) L
12:12 PM	(0.18) L	6:05 PM	(1.91) **H**	11:28 PM	(0.63) L
12:41 PM	(0.24) L	6:24 PM	(1.76) **H**	11:39 PM	(0.65) L
1:09 PM	(0.36) L	6:41 PM	(1.63) **H**	11:51 PM	(0.65) L
1:33 PM	(0.52) L	6:55 PM	(1.55) **H**		
7:00 AM	(2.58) **H**	1:49 PM	(0.68) L	7:07 PM	(1.54) **H**
7:21 AM	(2.43) **H**	1:59 PM	(0.78) L	7:24 PM	(1.56) **H**
7:45 AM	(2.25) **H**	2:13 PM	(0.87) L	7:49 PM	(1.55) **H**
8:11 AM	(2.01) **H**	2:42 PM	(0.98) L	8:26 PM	(1.47) **H**
8:33 AM	(1.69) **H**	3:36 PM	(1.17) L		
9:46 AM	(1.32) L	2:15 PM	(1.43) **H**	8:52 PM	(1.06) L
10:00 AM	(0.95) L	3:46 PM	(1.66) **H**	9:34 PM	(0.86) L
10:28 AM	(0.64) L	4:24 PM	(1.85) **H**	10:05 PM	(0.72) L
10:57 AM	(0.42) L	4:56 PM	(1.96) **H**	10:31 PM	(0.65) L
11:24 AM	(0.29) L	5:23 PM	(1.99) **H**	10:53 PM	(0.62) L
11:49 AM	(0.24) L	5:47 PM	(1.98) **H**	11:14 PM	(0.62) L
12:15 PM	(0.24) L	6:11 PM	(1.94) **H**	11:36 PM	(0.62) L
12:41 PM	(0.27) L	6:35 PM	(1.89) **H**	11:59 PM	(0.63) L
1:08 PM	(0.33) L	6:59 PM	(1.84) **H**		
6:51 AM	(2.60) **H**	1:34 PM	(0.41) L	7:21 PM	(1.79) **H**
7:17 AM	(2.52) **H**	1:59 PM	(0.48) L	7:45 PM	(1.74) **H**
7:42 AM	(2.42) **H**	2:27 PM	(0.56) L	8:13 PM	(1.70) **H**
8:13 AM	(2.29) **H**	3:02 PM	(0.65) L	8:56 PM	(1.64) **H**
8:53 AM	(2.08) **H**	3:53 PM	(0.79) L	10:12 PM	(1.56) **H**
10:02 AM	(1.80) **H**	5:27 PM	(0.94) L		
7:06 AM	(1.23) L	12:48 PM	(1.58) **H**	7:41 PM	(0.96) L

Adelaide Outer Harbour

POPULAR TIDE ADJUSTMENTS

Ardossan	-6min
Brighton	-4min
Cape Jervis	- 30min
Edithburgh	- 30min
Glenelg	-10min
Port Noarlunga	-15min
Port Stanvac	-7min
Port Wakefield	- 10min
Rapid Bay	- 5min
Second Valley	-3min
Port Vincent	- 30min

Day	Date		Tide 1
Mon	1		2:31 AM (1.89) **H**
Tue	2		3:27 AM (2.17) **H**
Wed	3		4:07 AM (2.40) **H**
Thu	4		4:40 AM (2.56) **H**
Fri	5	○	5:11 AM (2.66) **H**
Sat	6		5:40 AM (2.70) **H**
Sun	7		6:10 AM (2.69) **H**
Mon	8		6:41 AM (2.62) **H**
Tue	9		12:24 AM (0.73) L
Wed	10		12:54 AM (0.73) L
Thu	11		1:31 AM (0.77) L
Fri	12		2:16 AM (0.87) L
Sat	13		3:20 AM (1.02) L
Sun	14		5:05 AM (1.18) L
Mon	15		12:44 AM (1.89) **H**
Tue	16		2:25 AM (2.05) **H**
Wed	17		3:33 AM (2.25) **H**
Thu	18		4:20 AM (2.41) **H**
Fri	19		4:57 AM (2.51) **H**
Sat	20	●	5:30 AM (2.58) **H**
Sun	21		5:59 AM (2.62) **H**
Mon	22		12:03 AM (0.70) L
Tue	23		12:32 AM (0.67) L
Wed	24		1:02 AM (0.67) L
Thu	25		1:33 AM (0.69) L
Fri	26		2:09 AM (0.74) L
Sat	27		2:52 AM (0.81) L
Sun	28		3:49 AM (0.91) L
Mon	29		5:11 AM (1.03) L
Tue	30		12:03 AM (1.98) **H**
Wed	31		1:55 AM (2.03) **H**

DECEMBER 2025

Tide 2		Tide 3		Tide 4	
9:15 AM	(0.92) L	3:12 PM	(1.66) **H**	9:00 PM	(0.89) L
10:16 AM	(0.58) L	4:24 PM	(1.76) **H**	9:48 PM	(0.86) L
11:02 AM	(0.35) L	5:12 PM	(1.79) **H**	10:23 PM	(0.86) L
11:42 AM	(0.23) L	5:49 PM	(1.73) **H**	10:49 PM	(0.87) L
12:18 PM	(0.21) L	6:17 PM	(1.64) **H**	11:11 PM	(0.85) L
12:51 PM	(0.26) L	6:38 PM	(1.57) **H**	11:33 PM	(0.81) L
1:21 PM	(0.36) L	6:57 PM	(1.54) **H**	11:57 PM	(0.76) L
1:45 PM	(0.47) L	7:15 PM	(1.56) **H**		
7:09 AM	(2.51) **H**	2:03 PM	(0.57) L	7:36 PM	(1.62) **H**
7:36 AM	(2.38) **H**	2:18 PM	(0.62) L	8:04 PM	(1.71) **H**
8:04 AM	(2.23) **H**	2:37 PM	(0.64) L	8:42 PM	(1.78) **H**
8:38 AM	(2.05) **H**	3:06 PM	(0.67) L	9:36 PM	(1.82) **H**
9:22 AM	(1.81) **H**	3:49 PM	(0.77) L	10:55 PM	(1.83) **H**
10:36 AM	(1.54) **H**	4:56 PM	(0.92) L		
8:16 AM	(1.11) L	1:17 PM	(1.37) **H**	7:04 PM	(1.04) L
9:54 AM	(0.83) L	3:43 PM	(1.48) **H**	8:54 PM	(1.02) L
10:43 AM	(0.58) L	4:46 PM	(1.64) **H**	9:54 PM	(0.94) L
11:21 AM	(0.41) L	5:26 PM	(1.75) **H**	10:36 PM	(0.88) L
11:53 AM	(0.31) L	5:57 PM	(1.80) **H**	11:08 PM	(0.82) L
12:22 PM	(0.27) L	6:23 PM	(1.82) **H**	11:36 PM	(0.76) L
12:48 PM	(0.27) L	6:46 PM	(1.83) **H**		
6:27 AM	(2.63) **H**	1:14 PM	(0.28) L	7:09 PM	(1.84) **H**
6:55 AM	(2.61) **H**	1:40 PM	(0.30) L	7:35 PM	(1.85) **H**
7:24 AM	(2.55) **H**	2:06 PM	(0.33) L	8:02 PM	(1.87) **H**
7:52 AM	(2.46) **H**	2:32 PM	(0.37) L	8:32 PM	(1.89) **H**
8:22 AM	(2.34) **H**	2:59 PM	(0.43) L	9:08 PM	(1.93) **H**
8:57 AM	(2.16) **H**	3:29 PM	(0.52) L	9:53 PM	(1.96) **H**
9:41 AM	(1.91) **H**	4:05 PM	(0.67) L	10:50 PM	(1.97) **H**
10:41 AM	(1.60) **H**	4:45 PM	(0.87) L		
7:44 AM	(1.03) L	12:44 PM	(1.28) **H**	5:45 PM	(1.11) L
10:13 AM	(0.77) L	5:07 PM	(1.35) **H**	8:37 PM	(1.24) L

POPULAR TIDE ADJUSTMENTS

Ardossan	-6min
Brighton	-4min
Cape Jervis	- 30min
Edithburgh	- 30min
Glenelg	-10min
Port Noarlunga	-15min
Port Stanvac	-7min
Port Wakefield	- 10min
Rapid Bay	- 5min
Second Valley	-3min
Port Vincent	- 30min

Adelaide Outer Harbour

Day	Date	Tide 1
Thu	1	3:34 AM (2.19) **H**
Fri	2	4:37 AM (2.36) **H**
Sat	3 ○	5:22 AM (2.48) **H**
Sun	4	5:57 AM (2.56) **H**
Mon	5	6:26 AM (2.58) **H**
Tue	6	12:26 AM (0.74) L
Wed	7	12:55 AM (0.66) L
Thu	8	1:26 AM (0.62) L
Fri	9	2:00 AM (0.63) L
Sat	10	2:37 AM (0.68) L
Sun	11	3:19 AM (0.77) L
Mon	12	4:09 AM (0.91) L
Tue	13	5:19 AM (1.08) L
Wed	14	9:48 AM (1.10) L
Thu	15	2:35 AM (1.94) **H**
Fri	16	4:15 AM (2.12) **H**
Sat	17	5:05 AM (2.30) **H**
Sun	18	5:40 AM (2.44) **H**
Mon	19 ●	6:07 AM (2.54) **H**
Tue	20	12:15 AM (0.69) L
Wed	21	12:42 AM (0.59) L
Thu	22	1:11 AM (0.54) L
Fri	23	1:43 AM (0.53) L
Sat	24	2:15 AM (0.55) L
Sun	25	2:47 AM (0.59) L
Mon	26	3:24 AM (0.68) L
Tue	27	4:06 AM (0.83) L
Wed	28	5:09 AM (1.07) L
Thu	29	1:03 PM (0.78) L
Fri	30	3:55 AM (1.88) **H**
Sat	31	5:11 AM (2.16) **H**

Tide 2	Tide 3	Tide 4
11:19 AM (0.48) L	6:02 PM (1.50) **H**	10:06 PM (1.20) L
12:04 PM (0.30) L	6:34 PM (1.57) **H**	10:57 PM (1.10) L
12:40 PM (0.23) L	6:55 PM (1.59) **H**	11:30 PM (0.99) L
1:07 PM (0.25) L	7:06 PM (1.60) **H**	11:59 PM (0.86) L
1:29 PM (0.30) L	7:16 PM (1.66) **H**	
6:52 AM (2.55) **H**	1:44 PM (0.36) L	7:29 PM (1.76) **H**
7:17 AM (2.49) **H**	1:57 PM (0.39) L	7:48 PM (1.90) **H**
7:41 AM (2.40) **H**	2:10 PM (0.39) L	8:13 PM (2.04) **H**
8:06 AM (2.29) **H**	2:26 PM (0.37) L	8:44 PM (2.15) **H**
8:33 AM (2.15) **H**	2:47 PM (0.38) L	9:18 PM (2.22) **H**
9:04 AM (1.97) **H**	3:13 PM (0.45) L	10:00 PM (2.20) **H**
9:38 AM (1.73) **H**	3:40 PM (0.61) L	10:47 PM (2.12) **H**
10:17 AM (1.43) **H**	4:05 PM (0.85) L	11:58 PM (1.98) **H**
12:41 PM (1.12) **H**	2:53 PM (1.12) L	
11:05 AM (0.79) L	5:53 PM (1.41) **H**	9:36 PM (1.27) L
11:40 AM (0.53) L	6:04 PM (1.62) **H**	10:47 PM (1.10) L
12:09 PM (0.36) L	6:24 PM (1.75) **H**	11:25 PM (0.94) L
12:33 PM (0.27) L	6:42 PM (1.82) **H**	11:52 PM (0.81) L
12:54 PM (0.22) L	6:57 PM (1.87) **H**	
6:31 AM (2.60) **H**	1:13 PM (0.20) L	7:13 PM (1.94) **H**
6:56 AM (2.61) **H**	1:33 PM (0.19) L	7:33 PM (2.02) **H**
7:22 AM (2.57) **H**	1:54 PM (0.20) L	7:57 PM (2.10) **H**
7:47 AM (2.48) **H**	2:14 PM (0.23) L	8:21 PM (2.18) **H**
8:13 AM (2.34) **H**	2:31 PM (0.29) L	8:46 PM (2.26) **H**
8:37 AM (2.16) **H**	2:47 PM (0.36) L	9:13 PM (2.32) **H**
9:02 AM (1.94) **H**	3:01 PM (0.46) L	9:43 PM (2.31) **H**
9:24 AM (1.64) **H**	3:10 PM (0.61) L	10:17 PM (2.21) **H**
9:20 AM (1.30) **H**	2:53 PM (0.78) L	11:02 PM (1.99) **H**
12:16 PM (0.50) L	7:22 PM (1.60) **H**	11:08 PM (1.37) L
12:30 PM (0.28) L	7:07 PM (1.70) **H**	11:44 PM (1.11) L

POPULAR TIDE ADJUSTMENTS

Ardossan	-6min
Brighton	-4min
Cape Jervis	- 30min
Edithburgh	- 30min
Glenelg	-10min
Port Noarlunga	-15min
Port Stanvac	-7min
Port Wakefield	- 10min
Rapid Bay	- 5min
Second Valley	-3min
Port Vincent	- 30min

Adelaide Outer Harbour

Day	Date	Tide 1
Sun	1	5:49 AM (2.37) **H**
Mon	2 ○	12:06 AM (0.90) L
Tue	3	12:24 AM (0.72) L
Wed	4	12:42 AM (0.59) L
Thu	5	1:03 AM (0.50) L
Fri	6	1:29 AM (0.45) L
Sat	7	1:56 AM (0.46) L
Sun	8	2:24 AM (0.50) L
Mon	9	2:53 AM (0.58) L
Tue	10	3:24 AM (0.70) L
Wed	11	3:59 AM (0.90) L
Thu	12	4:48 AM (1.17) L
Fri	13	12:28 PM (0.82) L
Sat	14	4:39 AM (1.88) **H**
Sun	15	5:20 AM (2.17) **H**
Mon	16	5:47 AM (2.37) **H**
Tue	17 ●	12:02 AM (0.73) L
Wed	18	12:20 AM (0.59) L
Thu	19	12:41 AM (0.47) L
Fri	20	1:07 AM (0.39) L
Sat	21	1:35 AM (0.37) L
Sun	22	2:03 AM (0.40) L
Mon	23	2:28 AM (0.47) L
Tue	24	2:50 AM (0.57) L
Wed	25	3:13 AM (0.74) L
Thu	26	3:34 AM (1.01) L
Fri	27	3:26 AM (1.36) L
Sat	28*	1:04 AM (1.51) L

Day	Date	Tide 5
Sat	28	11:55 PM (1.23) L

* Additional Tide 5 - See Additional Tide 5

Tide 2		Tide 3		Tide 4	
12:49 PM	(0.20) L	7:07 PM	(1.75) **H**		
6:15 AM	(2.48) **H**	1:04 PM	(0.21) L	7:08 PM	(1.81) **H**
6:35 AM	(2.50) **H**	1:15 PM	(0.26) L	7:09 PM	(1.91) **H**
6:51 AM	(2.49) **H**	1:22 PM	(0.28) L	7:17 PM	(2.06) **H**
7:09 AM	(2.44) **H**	1:30 PM	(0.27) L	7:32 PM	(2.22) **H**
7:28 AM	(2.37) **H**	1:42 PM	(0.25) L	7:55 PM	(2.36) **H**
7:49 AM	(2.27) **H**	1:56 PM	(0.23) L	8:18 PM	(2.45) **H**
8:11 AM	(2.16) **H**	2:13 PM	(0.24) L	8:44 PM	(2.48) **H**
8:32 AM	(2.02) **H**	2:30 PM	(0.30) L	9:09 PM	(2.45) **H**
8:53 AM	(1.84) **H**	2:47 PM	(0.44) L	9:35 PM	(2.33) **H**
9:05 AM	(1.60) **H**	2:57 PM	(0.64) L	10:02 PM	(2.10) **H**
8:34 AM	(1.33) **H**	2:25 PM	(0.86) L	10:30 PM	(1.80) **H**
7:37 PM	(1.57) **H**	10:59 PM	(1.47) L		
12:01 PM	(0.56) L	6:37 PM	(1.70) **H**	11:23 PM	(1.16) L
12:13 PM	(0.35) L	6:33 PM	(1.85) **H**	11:44 PM	(0.92) L
12:29 PM	(0.24) L	6:41 PM	(1.95) **H**		
6:09 AM	(2.49) **H**	12:42 PM	(0.19) L	6:48 PM	(2.03) **H**
6:27 AM	(2.54) **H**	12:55 PM	(0.18) L	6:58 PM	(2.13) **H**
6:46 AM	(2.55) **H**	1:09 PM	(0.17) L	7:13 PM	(2.25) **H**
7:08 AM	(2.49) **H**	1:25 PM	(0.19) L	7:32 PM	(2.37) **H**
7:30 AM	(2.36) **H**	1:40 PM	(0.24) L	7:52 PM	(2.46) **H**
7:50 AM	(2.20) **H**	1:50 PM	(0.29) L	8:11 PM	(2.53) **H**
8:06 AM	(2.03) **H**	1:57 PM	(0.32) L	8:30 PM	(2.57) **H**
8:19 AM	(1.86) **H**	2:03 PM	(0.36) L	8:48 PM	(2.54) **H**
8:27 AM	(1.66) **H**	2:09 PM	(0.43) L	9:07 PM	(2.38) **H**
8:09 AM	(1.45) **H**	1:59 PM	(0.55) L	9:14 PM	(2.10) **H**
6:24 AM	(1.45) **H**	1:10 PM	(0.60) L	8:15 PM	(1.81) **H**
5:22 AM	(1.78) **H**	12:28 PM	(0.47) L	7:06 PM	(1.78) **H**

POPULAR TIDE ADJUSTMENTS

Ardossan	-6min
Brighton	-4min
Cape Jervis	- 30min
Edithburgh	- 30min
Glenelg	-10min
Port Noarlunga	-15min
Port Stanvac	-7min
Port Wakefield	- 10min
Rapid Bay	- 5min
Second Valley	-3min
Port Vincent	- 30min

Day	Date	Tide 5
Sun	15	11:23 PM (1.13) L
Sun	29	11:34 PM (1.12) L

Adelaide Outer Harbour

Day	Date	Tide 1
Sun	1	5:35 AM (2.11) **H**
Mon	2	5:55 AM (2.32) **H**
Tue	3 ○	12:09 AM (0.70) L
Wed	4	12:21 AM (0.55) L
Thu	5	12:34 AM (0.44) L
Fri	6	12:52 AM (0.38) L
Sat	7	1:15 AM (0.35) L
Sun	8	1:39 AM (0.38) L
Mon	9	2:03 AM (0.43) L
Tue	10	2:25 AM (0.50) L
Wed	11	2:46 AM (0.61) L
Thu	12	3:10 AM (0.78) L
Fri	13	3:33 AM (1.04) L
Sat	14	3:29 AM (1.39) L
Sun	15*	12:01 AM (1.46) L
Mon	16	5:11 AM (2.10) **H**
Tue	17	5:34 AM (2.32) **H**
Wed	18	5:53 AM (2.42) **H**
Thu	19 ●	12:09 AM (0.47) L
Fri	20	12:30 AM (0.36) L
Sat	21	12:54 AM (0.30) L
Sun	22	1:22 AM (0.30) L
Mon	23	1:47 AM (0.38) L
Tue	24	2:08 AM (0.49) L
Wed	25	2:22 AM (0.63) L
Thu	26	2:34 AM (0.79) L
Fri	27	2:44 AM (1.01) L
Sat	28	2:28 AM (1.28) L
Sun	29*	12:42 AM (1.39) L
Mon	30	5:17 AM (2.02) **H**
Tue	31	5:30 AM (2.20) **H**

* Additional Tide 5 - See Additional Tide 5

Tide 2			Tide 3			Tide 4		
12:21 PM	(0.31)	L	6:45 PM	(1.88)	**H**	11:57 PM	(0.92)	L
12:29 PM	(0.25)	L	6:41 PM	(1.98)	**H**			
6:12 AM	(2.41)	**H**	12:37 PM	(0.27)	L	6:40 PM	(2.07)	**H**
6:24 AM	(2.41)	**H**	12:41 PM	(0.30)	L	6:41 PM	(2.20)	**H**
6:34 AM	(2.38)	**H**	12:45 PM	(0.30)	L	6:48 PM	(2.35)	**H**
6:48 AM	(2.33)	**H**	12:53 PM	(0.28)	L	7:04 PM	(2.50)	**H**
7:06 AM	(2.26)	**H**	1:05 PM	(0.26)	L	7:25 PM	(2.60)	**H**
7:26 AM	(2.18)	**H**	1:20 PM	(0.27)	L	7:46 PM	(2.64)	**H**
7:45 AM	(2.08)	**H**	1:34 PM	(0.30)	L	8:07 PM	(2.63)	**H**
8:02 AM	(1.98)	**H**	1:50 PM	(0.34)	L	8:26 PM	(2.58)	**H**
8:18 AM	(1.86)	**H**	2:04 PM	(0.44)	L	8:45 PM	(2.46)	**H**
8:29 AM	(1.68)	**H**	2:13 PM	(0.60)	L	9:01 PM	(2.24)	**H**
8:16 AM	(1.46)	**H**	1:55 PM	(0.80)	L	9:01 PM	(1.93)	**H**
5:46 AM	(1.41)	**H**	12:32 PM	(0.85)	L	7:24 PM	(1.70)	**H**
4:48 AM	(1.77)	**H**	11:44 AM	(0.63)	L	6:17 PM	(1.80)	**H**
11:46 AM	(0.41)	L	6:07 PM	(1.98)	**H**	11:35 PM	(0.84)	L
11:59 AM	(0.30)	L	6:12 PM	(2.12)	**H**	11:51 PM	(0.63)	L
12:11 PM	(0.26)	L	6:18 PM	(2.24)	**H**			
6:11 AM	(2.44)	**H**	12:21 PM	(0.27)	L	6:27 PM	(2.38)	**H**
6:28 AM	(2.39)	**H**	12:32 PM	(0.29)	L	6:40 PM	(2.52)	**H**
6:47 AM	(2.29)	**H**	12:45 PM	(0.33)	L	6:59 PM	(2.63)	**H**
7:08 AM	(2.14)	**H**	12:57 PM	(0.38)	L	7:18 PM	(2.70)	**H**
7:25 AM	(1.97)	**H**	1:04 PM	(0.42)	L	7:36 PM	(2.72)	**H**
7:35 AM	(1.83)	**H**	1:08 PM	(0.41)	L	7:51 PM	(2.70)	**H**
7:43 AM	(1.73)	**H**	1:16 PM	(0.40)	L	8:08 PM	(2.61)	**H**
7:45 AM	(1.63)	**H**	1:25 PM	(0.45)	L	8:22 PM	(2.42)	**H**
7:30 AM	(1.53)	**H**	1:22 PM	(0.59)	L	8:21 PM	(2.12)	**H**
6:21 AM	(1.51)	**H**	12:43 PM	(0.72)	L	7:26 PM	(1.84)	**H**
5:19 AM	(1.74)	**H**	11:52 AM	(0.67)	L	6:21 PM	(1.83)	**H**
11:39 AM	(0.53)	L	5:57 PM	(2.01)	**H**	11:34 PM	(0.80)	L
11:44 AM	(0.45)	L	5:53 PM	(2.19)	**H**	11:47 PM	(0.58)	L

Adelaide Outer Harbour

POPULAR TIDE ADJUSTMENTS

Ardossan	-6min
Brighton	-4min
Cape Jervis	- 30min
Edithburgh	- 30min
Glenelg	-10min
Port Noarlunga	-15min
Port Stanvac	-7min
Port Wakefield	- 10min
Rapid Bay	- 5min
Second Valley	-3min
Port Vincent	- 30min

Day	Date	Tide 1
Wed	1	5:45 AM (2.27) **H**
Thu	2 ○	12:00 AM (0.45) L
Fri	3	12:15 AM (0.38) L
Sat	4	12:34 AM (0.33) L
Sun	5	12:57 AM (0.33) L
Mon	6	12:22 AM (0.37) L
Tue	7	12:45 AM (0.44) L
Wed	8	1:05 AM (0.53) L
Thu	9	1:25 AM (0.62) L
Fri	10	1:48 AM (0.76) L
Sat	11	2:17 AM (0.99) L
Sun	12	10:48 AM (1.08) L
Mon	13	2:45 AM (1.68) **H**
Tue	14	3:29 AM (2.00) **H**
Wed	15	4:00 AM (2.21) **H**
Thu	16	4:25 AM (2.29) **H**
Fri	17 ●	4:46 AM (2.26) **H**
Sat	18	5:07 AM (2.18) **H**
Sun	19	5:29 AM (2.05) **H**
Mon	20	12:11 AM (0.33) L
Tue	21	12:38 AM (0.45) L
Wed	22	12:59 AM (0.61) L
Thu	23	1:12 AM (0.76) L
Fri	24	1:22 AM (0.90) L
Sat	25	1:38 AM (1.05) L
Sun	26*	1:53 AM (1.27) L
Mon	27	3:16 AM (1.55) **H**
Tue	28	3:21 AM (1.80) **H**
Wed	29	3:45 AM (1.98) **H**
Thu	30	4:06 AM (2.08) **H**

Day	Date	Tide 5
Sun	26	11:33 PM (1.47) L

* Additional Tide 5 - See Additional Tide 5

Tide 2		Tide 3		Tide 4	
11:50 AM	(0.43) L	5:56 PM	(2.34) **H**		
5:58 AM	(2.27) **H**	11:55 AM	(0.43) L	6:02 PM	(2.48) **H**
6:09 AM	(2.24) **H**	12:01 PM	(0.41) L	6:14 PM	(2.62) **H**
6:24 AM	(2.20) **H**	12:13 PM	(0.39) L	6:32 PM	(2.72) **H**
5:45 AM	(2.14) **H**	11:30 AM	(0.40) L	5:55 PM	(2.75) **H**
6:06 AM	(2.06) **H**	11:46 AM	(0.43) L	6:17 PM	(2.74) **H**
6:26 AM	(1.97) **H**	12:03 PM	(0.47) L	6:37 PM	(2.69) **H**
6:43 AM	(1.90) **H**	12:19 PM	(0.52) L	6:56 PM	(2.62) **H**
7:00 AM	(1.82) **H**	12:36 PM	(0.59) L	7:15 PM	(2.50) **H**
7:15 AM	(1.69) **H**	12:50 PM	(0.74) L	7:36 PM	(2.29) **H**
7:24 AM	(1.48) **H**	12:45 PM	(0.96) L	7:49 PM	(1.98) **H**
5:59 PM	(1.67) **H**	10:22 PM	(1.54) L		
9:42 AM	(0.84) L	4:21 PM	(1.83) **H**	9:43 PM	(1.16) L
9:52 AM	(0.61) L	4:15 PM	(2.09) **H**	10:02 PM	(0.82) L
10:09 AM	(0.49) L	4:24 PM	(2.31) **H**	10:26 PM	(0.57) L
10:25 AM	(0.46) L	4:35 PM	(2.48) **H**	10:49 PM	(0.40) L
10:37 AM	(0.49) L	4:47 PM	(2.63) **H**	11:14 PM	(0.31) L
10:50 AM	(0.52) L	5:05 PM	(2.76) **H**	11:41 PM	(0.28) L
11:03 AM	(0.55) L	5:27 PM	(2.84) **H**		
5:50 AM	(1.90) **H**	11:15 AM	(0.59) L	5:50 PM	(2.84) **H**
6:07 AM	(1.75) **H**	11:25 AM	(0.61) L	6:11 PM	(2.79) **H**
6:17 AM	(1.65) **H**	11:34 AM	(0.60) L	6:30 PM	(2.69) **H**
6:27 AM	(1.61) **H**	11:48 AM	(0.61) L	6:48 PM	(2.55) **H**
6:37 AM	(1.59) **H**	12:06 PM	(0.69) L	7:07 PM	(2.33) **H**
6:42 AM	(1.51) **H**	12:16 PM	(0.89) L	7:16 PM	(2.02) **H**
5:39 AM	(1.40) **H**	11:15 AM	(1.12) L	6:03 PM	(1.71) **H**
9:26 AM	(1.05) L	4:05 PM	(1.78) **H**	9:42 PM	(1.17) L
9:25 AM	(0.86) L	3:44 PM	(2.09) **H**	9:53 PM	(0.84) L
9:38 AM	(0.72) L	3:52 PM	(2.36) **H**	10:14 PM	(0.61) L
9:53 AM	(0.65) L	4:07 PM	(2.56) **H**	10:34 PM	(0.47) L

POPULAR TIDE ADJUSTMENTS

Ardossan	-6min
Brighton	-4min
Cape Jervis	- 30min
Edithburgh	- 30min
Glenelg	-10min
Port Noarlunga	-15min
Port Stanvac	-7min
Port Wakefield	- 10min
Rapid Bay	- 5min
Second Valley	-3min
Port Vincent	- 30min

Adelaide Outer Harbour

Day	Date	Tide 1
Fri	1	4:26 AM (2.11) **H**
Sat	2 ○	4:45 AM (2.10) **H**
Sun	3	5:06 AM (2.07) **H**
Mon	4	5:31 AM (2.03) **H**
Tue	5	12:11 AM (0.42) L
Wed	6	12:37 AM (0.50) L
Thu	7	1:00 AM (0.58) L
Fri	8	1:25 AM (0.66) L
Sat	9	1:55 AM (0.77) L
Sun	10	2:41 AM (0.92) L
Mon	11	4:28 AM (1.09) L
Tue	12	7:19 AM (1.03) L
Wed	13	2:06 AM (1.86) **H**
Thu	14	3:11 AM (2.01) **H**
Fri	15	3:54 AM (2.07) **H**
Sat	16	4:27 AM (2.03) **H**
Sun	17 ●	4:55 AM (1.93) **H**
Mon	18	5:21 AM (1.81) **H**
Tue	19	12:10 AM (0.42) L
Wed	20	12:42 AM (0.55) L
Thu	21	1:07 AM (0.70) L
Fri	22	1:25 AM (0.82) L
Sat	23	1:42 AM (0.90) L
Sun	24	2:09 AM (0.97) L
Mon	25	3:00 AM (1.07) L
Tue	26	5:04 AM (1.15) L
Wed	27	12:56 AM (1.60) **H**
Thu	28	2:33 AM (1.73) **H**
Fri	29	3:25 AM (1.86) **H**
Sat	30	4:02 AM (1.93) **H**
Sun	31 ○	4:33 AM (1.96) **H**

Tide 2		Tide 3		Tide 4	
10:06 AM	(0.61) L	4:23 PM	(2.70) **H**	10:55 PM	(0.39) L
10:21 AM	(0.59) L	4:43 PM	(2.79) **H**	11:17 PM	(0.37) L
10:41 AM	(0.58) L	5:06 PM	(2.84) **H**	11:44 PM	(0.38) L
11:03 AM	(0.60) L	5:32 PM	(2.83) **H**		
5:57 AM	(1.97) **H**	11:26 AM	(0.64) L	5:59 PM	(2.78) **H**
6:21 AM	(1.91) **H**	11:47 AM	(0.68) L	6:22 PM	(2.71) **H**
6:42 AM	(1.85) **H**	12:08 PM	(0.73) L	6:45 PM	(2.62) **H**
7:05 AM	(1.80) **H**	12:31 PM	(0.81) L	7:10 PM	(2.50) **H**
7:35 AM	(1.71) **H**	12:58 PM	(0.95) L	7:41 PM	(2.31) **H**
8:27 AM	(1.57) **H**	1:29 PM	(1.18) L	8:28 PM	(2.03) **H**
12:30 PM	(1.51) **H**	2:20 PM	(1.50) L	11:23 PM	(1.74) **H**
2:25 PM	(1.85) **H**	8:26 PM	(1.22) L		
8:26 AM	(0.86) L	2:58 PM	(2.18) **H**	9:16 PM	(0.85) L
9:04 AM	(0.77) L	3:25 PM	(2.44) **H**	9:55 PM	(0.58) L
9:32 AM	(0.75) L	3:49 PM	(2.64) **H**	10:30 PM	(0.41) L
9:54 AM	(0.77) L	4:13 PM	(2.78) **H**	11:02 PM	(0.34) L
10:13 AM	(0.79) L	4:39 PM	(2.88) **H**	11:36 PM	(0.35) L
10:32 AM	(0.80) L	5:07 PM	(2.91) **H**		
5:46 AM	(1.71) **H**	10:52 AM	(0.81) L	5:37 PM	(2.87) **H**
6:08 AM	(1.63) **H**	11:11 AM	(0.81) L	6:05 PM	(2.77) **H**
6:26 AM	(1.60) **H**	11:31 AM	(0.82) L	6:30 PM	(2.63) **H**
6:46 AM	(1.62) **H**	11:58 AM	(0.85) L	6:56 PM	(2.47) **H**
7:16 AM	(1.66) **H**	12:34 PM	(0.95) L	7:26 PM	(2.27) **H**
8:07 AM	(1.67) **H**	1:22 PM	(1.15) L	8:05 PM	(2.01) **H**
9:56 AM	(1.66) **H**	3:01 PM	(1.42) L	9:30 PM	(1.70) **H**
12:44 PM	(1.86) **H**	7:57 PM	(1.30) L		
7:11 AM	(1.09) L	2:00 PM	(2.16) **H**	9:00 PM	(0.99) L
8:13 AM	(0.97) L	2:47 PM	(2.42) **H**	9:38 PM	(0.74) L
8:55 AM	(0.89) L	3:23 PM	(2.62) **H**	10:11 PM	(0.57) L
9:27 AM	(0.84) L	3:54 PM	(2.74) **H**	10:41 PM	(0.48) L
9:56 AM	(0.81) L	4:23 PM	(2.81) **H**	11:10 PM	(0.45) L

POPULAR TIDE ADJUSTMENTS

Ardossan	-6min
Brighton	-4min
Cape Jervis	- 30min
Edithburgh	- 30min
Glenelg	-10min
Port Noarlunga	-15min
Port Stanvac	-7min
Port Wakefield	- 10min
Rapid Bay	- 5min
Second Valley	-3min
Port Vincent	- 30min

Adelaide Outer Harbour

Day	Date	Tide 1
Mon	1	5:01 AM (1.97) **H**
Tue	2	5:30 AM (1.96) **H**
Wed	3	12:08 AM (0.47) L
Thu	4	12:36 AM (0.52) L
Fri	5	1:04 AM (0.57) L
Sat	6	1:32 AM (0.62) L
Sun	7	2:04 AM (0.67) L
Mon	8	2:45 AM (0.74) L
Tue	9	3:41 AM (0.86) L
Wed	10	4:58 AM (0.98) L
Thu	11	12:16 AM (1.73) **H**
Fri	12	2:16 AM (1.73) **H**
Sat	13	3:36 AM (1.77) **H**
Sun	14	4:30 AM (1.76) **H**
Mon	15 ●	5:09 AM (1.72) **H**
Tue	16	5:38 AM (1.67) **H**
Wed	17	12:20 AM (0.48) L
Thu	18	12:49 AM (0.57) L
Fri	19	1:12 AM (0.66) L
Sat	20	1:28 AM (0.72) L
Sun	21	1:44 AM (0.73) L
Mon	22	2:06 AM (0.73) L
Tue	23	2:39 AM (0.76) L
Wed	24	3:24 AM (0.86) L
Thu	25	4:28 AM (1.02) L
Fri	26	12:51 AM (1.50) **H**
Sat	27	3:00 AM (1.60) **H**
Sun	28	4:02 AM (1.74) **H**
Mon	29	4:42 AM (1.84) **H**
Tue	30 ○	5:12 AM (1.89) **H**

Tide 2		Tide 3		Tide 4	
10:23 AM	(0.78) L	4:53 PM	(2.84) **H**	11:38 PM	(0.45) L
10:52 AM	(0.77) L	5:23 PM	(2.83) **H**		
5:58 AM	(1.94) **H**	11:20 AM	(0.78) L	5:52 PM	(2.79) **H**
6:26 AM	(1.92) **H**	11:49 AM	(0.81) L	6:20 PM	(2.73) **H**
6:54 AM	(1.90) **H**	12:17 PM	(0.85) L	6:47 PM	(2.64) **H**
7:24 AM	(1.89) **H**	12:49 PM	(0.92) L	7:17 PM	(2.54) **H**
8:04 AM	(1.89) **H**	1:30 PM	(1.01) L	7:54 PM	(2.38) **H**
9:00 AM	(1.89) **H**	2:30 PM	(1.15) L	8:45 PM	(2.16) **H**
10:18 AM	(1.91) **H**	4:12 PM	(1.28) L	10:09 PM	(1.91) **H**
11:58 AM	(2.03) **H**	6:41 PM	(1.21) L		
6:33 AM	(1.05) L	1:24 PM	(2.23) **H**	8:28 PM	(0.95) L
7:49 AM	(1.06) L	2:27 PM	(2.45) **H**	9:33 PM	(0.68) L
8:44 AM	(1.07) L	3:15 PM	(2.62) **H**	10:24 PM	(0.50) L
9:24 AM	(1.07) L	3:56 PM	(2.75) **H**	11:07 PM	(0.42) L
9:57 AM	(1.05) L	4:32 PM	(2.82) **H**	11:45 PM	(0.42) L
10:27 AM	(1.00) L	5:07 PM	(2.84) **H**		
6:01 AM	(1.65) **H**	10:57 AM	(0.95) L	5:40 PM	(2.81) **H**
6:23 AM	(1.67) **H**	11:28 AM	(0.91) L	6:11 PM	(2.72) **H**
6:45 AM	(1.74) **H**	12:00 PM	(0.89) L	6:38 PM	(2.60) **H**
7:11 AM	(1.84) **H**	12:36 PM	(0.91) L	7:06 PM	(2.46) **H**
7:45 AM	(1.97) **H**	1:19 PM	(0.96) L	7:36 PM	(2.31) **H**
8:30 AM	(2.07) **H**	2:13 PM	(1.06) L	8:14 PM	(2.12) **H**
9:26 AM	(2.13) **H**	3:23 PM	(1.19) L	9:04 PM	(1.89) **H**
10:36 AM	(2.15) **H**	5:10 PM	(1.28) L	10:24 PM	(1.63) **H**
12:09 PM	(2.20) **H**	7:48 PM	(1.17) L		
6:18 AM	(1.15) L	1:45 PM	(2.31) **H**	9:15 PM	(0.93) L
8:03 AM	(1.15) L	2:53 PM	(2.47) **H**	10:05 PM	(0.72) L
9:06 AM	(1.08) L	3:42 PM	(2.60) **H**	10:44 PM	(0.58) L
9:50 AM	(1.00) L	4:20 PM	(2.69) **H**	11:15 PM	(0.51) L
10:24 AM	(0.92) L	4:52 PM	(2.75) **H**	11:43 PM	(0.48) L

POPULAR TIDE ADJUSTMENTS

Ardossan	-6min
Brighton	-4min
Cape Jervis	- 30min
Edithburgh	- 30min
Glenelg	-10min
Port Noarlunga	-15min
Port Stanvac	-7min
Port Wakefield	- 10min
Rapid Bay	- 5min
Second Valley	-3min
Port Vincent	- 30min

Adelaide Outer Harbour

Day	Date	Tide 1
Wed	1	5:36 AM (1.93) **H**
Thu	2	12:08 AM (0.47) L
Fri	3	12:33 AM (0.47) L
Sat	4	12:59 AM (0.48) L
Sun	5	1:24 AM (0.50) L
Mon	6	1:50 AM (0.52) L
Tue	7	2:17 AM (0.57) L
Wed	8	2:48 AM (0.67) L
Thu	9	3:23 AM (0.83) L
Fri	10	4:03 AM (1.05) L
Sat	11	1:20 AM (1.36) **H**
Sun	12	4:40 AM (1.51) **H**
Mon	13	5:20 AM (1.64) **H**
Tue	14 ●	5:45 AM (1.69) **H**
Wed	15	6:01 AM (1.71) **H**
Thu	16	12:22 AM (0.45) L
Fri	17	12:39 AM (0.51) L
Sat	18	12:52 AM (0.56) L
Sun	19	1:03 AM (0.56) L
Mon	20	1:15 AM (0.54) L
Tue	21	1:33 AM (0.51) L
Wed	22	1:57 AM (0.53) L
Thu	23	2:24 AM (0.63) L
Fri	24	2:53 AM (0.84) L
Sat	25	3:17 AM (1.11) L
Sun	26	5:20 AM (1.41) **H**
Mon	27	4:43 AM (1.65) **H**
Tue	28	5:04 AM (1.81) **H**
Wed	29	5:24 AM (1.91) **H**
Thu	30 ○	5:39 AM (1.97) **H**
Fri	31	5:55 AM (2.03) **H**

Tide 2		Tide 3		Tide 4	
10:54 AM	(0.85) L	5:21 PM	(2.78) **H**		
6:00 AM	(1.96) **H**	11:24 AM	(0.80) L	5:49 PM	(2.78) **H**
6:27 AM	(1.99) **H**	11:55 AM	(0.78) L	6:17 PM	(2.74) **H**
6:55 AM	(2.03) **H**	12:28 PM	(0.80) L	6:45 PM	(2.67) **H**
7:26 AM	(2.08) **H**	1:02 PM	(0.83) L	7:15 PM	(2.57) **H**
7:59 AM	(2.15) **H**	1:43 PM	(0.88) L	7:46 PM	(2.43) **H**
8:36 AM	(2.21) **H**	2:30 PM	(0.95) L	8:24 PM	(2.23) **H**
9:21 AM	(2.25) **H**	3:30 PM	(1.05) L	9:10 PM	(1.96) **H**
10:15 AM	(2.24) **H**	4:58 PM	(1.16) L	10:15 PM	(1.63) **H**
11:33 AM	(2.21) **H**	7:51 PM	(1.10) L		
5:07 AM	(1.29) L	1:37 PM	(2.26) **H**	9:51 PM	(0.81) L
8:14 AM	(1.37) L	3:10 PM	(2.43) **H**	10:47 PM	(0.56) L
9:30 AM	(1.28) L	4:07 PM	(2.59) **H**	11:28 PM	(0.43) L
10:16 AM	(1.15) L	4:47 PM	(2.70) **H**	11:59 PM	(0.40) L
10:49 AM	(1.02) L	5:19 PM	(2.74) **H**		
6:11 AM	(1.76) **H**	11:17 AM	(0.90) L	5:45 PM	(2.72) **H**
6:23 AM	(1.86) **H**	11:47 AM	(0.81) L	6:09 PM	(2.65) **H**
6:39 AM	(1.99) **H**	12:17 PM	(0.77) L	6:32 PM	(2.55) **H**
7:02 AM	(2.15) **H**	12:49 PM	(0.77) L	6:55 PM	(2.44) **H**
7:30 AM	(2.28) **H**	1:24 PM	(0.80) L	7:19 PM	(2.32) **H**
8:02 AM	(2.38) **H**	2:01 PM	(0.87) L	7:46 PM	(2.17) **H**
8:40 AM	(2.41) **H**	2:45 PM	(0.98) L	8:17 PM	(1.98) **H**
9:22 AM	(2.34) **H**	3:39 PM	(1.14) L	8:51 PM	(1.72) **H**
10:17 AM	(2.20) **H**	5:26 PM	(1.31) L	9:31 PM	(1.41) **H**
12:15 PM	(2.05) **H**	9:52 PM	(1.08) L		
7:22 AM	(1.39) L	2:49 PM	(2.19) **H**	10:27 PM	(0.80) L
9:21 AM	(1.23) L	3:51 PM	(2.40) **H**	10:57 PM	(0.59) L
10:08 AM	(1.05) L	4:29 PM	(2.56) **H**	11:21 PM	(0.47) L
10:37 AM	(0.91) L	4:57 PM	(2.66) **H**	11:41 PM	(0.43) L
11:00 AM	(0.80) L	5:20 PM	(2.71) **H**	11:59 PM	(0.41) L
11:24 AM	(0.71) L	5:42 PM	(2.73) **H**		

POPULAR TIDE ADJUSTMENTS

Ardossan	-6min
Brighton	-4min
Cape Jervis	- 30min
Edithburgh	- 30min
Glenelg	-10min
Port Noarlunga	-15min
Port Stanvac	-7min
Port Wakefield	- 10min
Rapid Bay	- 5min
Second Valley	-3min
Port Vincent	- 30min

Adelaide Outer Harbour

Day	Date	Tide 1
Sat	1	12:15 AM (0.39) L
Sun	2	12:35 AM (0.38) L
Mon	3	12:56 AM (0.40) L
Tue	4	1:15 AM (0.44) L
Wed	5	1:31 AM (0.48) L
Thu	6	1:48 AM (0.56) L
Fri	7	2:02 AM (0.68) L
Sat	8	2:03 AM (0.86) L
Sun	9	12:43 AM (0.98) L
Mon	10	6:13 AM (1.63) **H**
Tue	11	5:46 AM (1.75) **H**
Wed	12	5:48 AM (1.84) **H**
Thu	13 ●	5:51 AM (1.89) **H**
Fri	14	12:00 AM (0.40) L
Sat	15	12:08 AM (0.46) L
Sun	16	12:14 AM (0.47) L
Mon	17	12:23 AM (0.45) L
Tue	18	12:35 AM (0.42) L
Wed	19	12:50 AM (0.41) L
Thu	20	1:09 AM (0.43) L
Fri	21	1:29 AM (0.53) L
Sat	22	1:45 AM (0.71) L
Sun	23	1:34 AM (0.95) L
Mon	24	6:31 AM (1.56) **H**
Tue	25	5:07 AM (1.71) **H**
Wed	26	5:04 AM (1.89) **H**
Thu	27	5:14 AM (2.01) **H**
Fri	28 ○	5:23 AM (2.09) **H**
Sat	29	5:31 AM (2.17) **H**
Sun	30	5:45 AM (2.29) **H**
Mon	31	12:00 AM (0.35) L

Tide 2			Tide 3			Tide 4		
6:13 AM	(2.11)	**H**	11:52 AM	(0.65)	L	6:05 PM	(2.69)	**H**
6:36 AM	(2.20)	**H**	12:23 PM	(0.64)	L	6:30 PM	(2.61)	**H**
7:02 AM	(2.28)	**H**	12:55 PM	(0.66)	L	6:55 PM	(2.49)	**H**
7:28 AM	(2.36)	**H**	1:28 PM	(0.70)	L	7:19 PM	(2.34)	**H**
7:54 AM	(2.43)	**H**	2:01 PM	(0.77)	L	7:44 PM	(2.14)	**H**
8:23 AM	(2.44)	**H**	2:40 PM	(0.89)	L	8:08 PM	(1.89)	**H**
8:57 AM	(2.37)	**H**	3:30 PM	(1.10)	L	8:22 PM	(1.57)	**H**
9:40 AM	(2.17)	**H**						
1:48 PM	(1.93)	**H**	11:04 PM	(0.75)	L			
9:26 AM	(1.50)	L	3:49 PM	(2.24)	**H**	11:11 PM	(0.48)	L
10:19 AM	(1.21)	L	4:32 PM	(2.49)	**H**	11:31 PM	(0.34)	L
10:47 AM	(0.98)	L	5:01 PM	(2.62)	**H**	11:49 PM	(0.34)	L
11:08 AM	(0.81)	L	5:22 PM	(2.64)	**H**			
5:53 AM	(1.96)	**H**	11:26 AM	(0.69)	L	5:38 PM	(2.60)	**H**
5:59 AM	(2.10)	**H**	11:45 AM	(0.61)	L	5:53 PM	(2.53)	**H**
6:12 AM	(2.25)	**H**	12:09 PM	(0.58)	L	6:10 PM	(2.44)	**H**
6:32 AM	(2.39)	**H**	12:36 PM	(0.59)	L	6:29 PM	(2.33)	**H**
6:57 AM	(2.49)	**H**	1:03 PM	(0.64)	L	6:49 PM	(2.23)	**H**
7:23 AM	(2.53)	**H**	1:30 PM	(0.71)	L	7:10 PM	(2.11)	**H**
7:49 AM	(2.51)	**H**	2:00 PM	(0.82)	L	7:30 PM	(1.96)	**H**
8:17 AM	(2.40)	**H**	2:32 PM	(0.99)	L	7:46 PM	(1.76)	**H**
8:48 AM	(2.18)	**H**	3:15 PM	(1.25)	L	7:32 PM	(1.51)	**H**
9:30 AM	(1.88)	**H**	11:29 PM	(1.01)	L			
9:06 AM	(1.53)	L	3:21 PM	(1.95)	**H**	10:42 PM	(0.76)	L
9:55 AM	(1.20)	L	4:03 PM	(2.26)	**H**	10:52 PM	(0.53)	L
10:21 AM	(0.94)	L	4:31 PM	(2.47)	**H**	11:08 PM	(0.40)	L
10:42 AM	(0.76)	L	4:53 PM	(2.58)	**H**	11:22 PM	(0.36)	L
10:59 AM	(0.64)	L	5:09 PM	(2.61)	**H**	11:33 PM	(0.35)	L
11:17 AM	(0.54)	L	5:26 PM	(2.60)	**H**	11:45 PM	(0.35)	L
11:41 AM	(0.48)	L	5:45 PM	(2.55)	**H**			
6:03 AM	(2.39)	**H**	12:09 PM	(0.46)	L	6:06 PM	(2.44)	**H**

Adelaide Outer Harbour

Day	Date	Tide 1
Tue	1	12:15 AM (0.39) L
Wed	2	12:29 AM (0.44) L
Thu	3	12:38 AM (0.47) L
Fri	4	12:45 AM (0.50) L
Sat	5	12:53 AM (0.57) L
Sun	6	12:47 AM (0.68) L
Mon	7*	12:00 AM (0.76) L
Tue	8	5:41 AM (1.75) **H**
Wed	9	5:16 AM (1.89) **H**
Thu	10	5:15 AM (2.02) **H**
Fri	11 ●	5:15 AM (2.11) **H**
Sat	12	5:17 AM (2.22) **H**
Sun	13	5:22 AM (2.36) **H**
Mon	14	5:36 AM (2.50) **H**
Tue	15	5:57 AM (2.58) **H**
Wed	16	6:20 AM (2.61) **H**
Thu	17	12:09 AM (0.41) L
Fri	18	12:26 AM (0.45) L
Sat	19	12:44 AM (0.54) L
Sun	20	12:56 AM (0.69) L
Mon	21*	12:45 AM (0.89) L
Tue	22	5:56 AM (1.62) **H**
Wed	23	4:40 AM (1.76) **H**
Thu	24	4:32 AM (1.98) **H**
Fri	25	4:41 AM (2.14) **H**
Sat	26	4:49 AM (2.26) **H**
Sun	27 ○	4:58 AM (2.38) **H**
Mon	28	5:10 AM (2.50) **H**
Tue	29	5:29 AM (2.60) **H**
Wed	30	5:50 AM (2.65) **H**

* Additional Tide 5 - See Additional Tide 5

POPULAR TIDE ADJUSTMENTS

Ardossan	-6min
Brighton	-4min
Cape Jervis	- 30min
Edithburgh	- 30min
Glenelg	-10min
Port Noarlunga	-15min
Port Stanvac	-7min
Port Wakefield	- 10min
Rapid Bay	- 5min
Second Valley	-3min
Port Vincent	- 30min

Day	Date	Tide 5
Mon	7	11:05 PM (0.63) L
Mon	21	11:15 PM (0.97) L

SEPTEMBER 2026

Tide 2		Tide 3		Tide 4	
6:26 AM	(2.47) **H**	12:37 PM	(0.50) L	6:28 PM	(2.28) **H**
6:47 AM	(2.53) **H**	1:03 PM	(0.57) L	6:45 PM	(2.12) **H**
7:07 AM	(2.55) **H**	1:27 PM	(0.67) L	7:00 PM	(1.95) **H**
7:28 AM	(2.52) **H**	1:49 PM	(0.82) L	7:10 PM	(1.77) **H**
7:49 AM	(2.39) **H**	2:12 PM	(1.06) L	7:01 PM	(1.56) **H**
8:03 AM	(2.12) **H**	2:15 PM	(1.39) L	5:19 PM	(1.48) **H**
7:10 AM	(1.80) **H**	11:47 AM	(1.59) L	3:55 PM	(1.81) **H**
10:19 AM	(1.29) L	4:11 PM	(2.17) **H**	10:56 PM	(0.44) L
10:29 AM	(0.94) L	4:34 PM	(2.41) **H**	11:06 PM	(0.34) L
10:45 AM	(0.70) L	4:54 PM	(2.50) **H**	11:16 PM	(0.35) L
11:00 AM	(0.55) L	5:07 PM	(2.48) **H**	11:21 PM	(0.41) L
11:15 AM	(0.47) L	5:16 PM	(2.41) **H**	11:23 PM	(0.44) L
11:30 AM	(0.42) L	5:27 PM	(2.34) **H**	11:29 PM	(0.42) L
11:51 AM	(0.41) L	5:42 PM	(2.26) **H**	11:39 PM	(0.40) L
12:15 PM	(0.45) L	6:00 PM	(2.17) **H**	11:53 PM	(0.39) L
12:38 PM	(0.52) L	6:20 PM	(2.08) **H**		
6:43 AM	(2.58) **H**	1:00 PM	(0.61) L	6:39 PM	(1.98) **H**
7:04 AM	(2.51) **H**	1:21 PM	(0.71) L	6:55 PM	(1.88) **H**
7:25 AM	(2.38) **H**	1:44 PM	(0.87) L	7:07 PM	(1.73) **H**
7:45 AM	(2.17) **H**	2:07 PM	(1.10) L	6:58 PM	(1.53) **H**
7:49 AM	(1.87) **H**	2:00 PM	(1.42) L	4:39 PM	(1.46) **H**
10:08 AM	(1.45) L	3:28 PM	(1.80) **H**	10:17 PM	(0.76) L
9:51 AM	(1.10) L	3:50 PM	(2.12) **H**	10:21 PM	(0.53) L
10:08 AM	(0.80) L	4:14 PM	(2.35) **H**	10:34 PM	(0.40) L
10:28 AM	(0.59) L	4:33 PM	(2.44) **H**	10:46 PM	(0.36) L
10:45 AM	(0.45) L	4:50 PM	(2.45) **H**	10:56 PM	(0.37) L
11:04 AM	(0.36) L	5:05 PM	(2.40) **H**	11:06 PM	(0.38) L
11:28 AM	(0.30) L	5:23 PM	(2.31) **H**	11:19 PM	(0.40) L
11:54 AM	(0.31) L	5:44 PM	(2.18) **H**	11:32 PM	(0.45) L
12:21 PM	(0.39) L	6:03 PM	(2.01) **H**	11:43 PM	(0.50) L

POPULAR TIDE ADJUSTMENTS

Ardossan	-6min
Brighton	-4min
Cape Jervis	- 30min
Edithburgh	- 30min
Glenelg	-10min
Port Noarlunga	-15min
Port Stanvac	-7min
Port Wakefield	- 10min
Rapid Bay	- 5min
Second Valley	-3min
Port Vincent	- 30min

Day	Date	Tide 5
Tue	6	11:25 PM (0.75) L
Tue	20	11:34 PM (1.14) L

Adelaide Outer Harbour

Day	Date	Tide 1
Thu	1	6:11 AM (2.64) **H**
Fri	2	6:29 AM (2.59) **H**
Sat	3	6:46 AM (2.50) **H**
Sun	4	12:04 AM (0.56) L
Mon	5	1:02 AM (0.68) L
Tue	6*	12:22 AM (0.80) L
Wed	7	5:49 AM (1.76) **H**
Thu	8	5:25 AM (1.96) **H**
Fri	9	5:25 AM (2.17) **H**
Sat	10	5:30 AM (2.33) **H**
Sun	11 ●	5:37 AM (2.47) **H**
Mon	12	5:47 AM (2.59) **H**
Tue	13	6:05 AM (2.68) **H**
Wed	14	12:04 AM (0.43) L
Thu	15	12:23 AM (0.46) L
Fri	16	12:42 AM (0.51) L
Sat	17	1:00 AM (0.56) L
Sun	18	1:18 AM (0.64) L
Mon	19	1:35 AM (0.78) L
Tue	20*	1:37 AM (0.99) L
Wed	21	6:33 AM (1.55) **H**
Thu	22	4:40 AM (1.74) **H**
Fri	23	4:40 AM (2.03) **H**
Sat	24	4:54 AM (2.26) **H**
Sun	25	5:08 AM (2.43) **H**
Mon	26 ○	5:22 AM (2.57) **H**
Tue	27	5:40 AM (2.68) **H**
Wed	28	6:02 AM (2.75) **H**
Thu	29	12:00 AM (0.58) L
Fri	30	12:13 AM (0.62) L
Sat	31	12:22 AM (0.64) L

* Additional Tide 5 - See Additional Tide 5

Tide 2		Tide 3		Tide 4	
12:45 PM	(0.52) L	6:16 PM	(1.85) **H**	11:49 PM	(0.52) L
1:00 PM	(0.66) L	6:25 PM	(1.72) **H**	11:56 PM	(0.52) L
1:13 PM	(0.82) L	6:29 PM	(1.62) **H**		
8:02 AM	(2.32) **H**	2:23 PM	(1.03) L	7:15 PM	(1.52) **H**
8:05 AM	(2.03) **H**	2:10 PM	(1.29) L	6:01 PM	(1.49) **H**
7:03 AM	(1.75) **H**	12:16 PM	(1.40) L	4:53 PM	(1.72) **H**
11:00 AM	(1.10) L	4:53 PM	(2.01) **H**	11:12 PM	(0.59) L
11:07 AM	(0.75) L	5:11 PM	(2.20) **H**	11:20 PM	(0.49) L
11:24 AM	(0.51) L	5:28 PM	(2.27) **H**	11:29 PM	(0.46) L
11:41 AM	(0.38) L	5:41 PM	(2.25) **H**	11:33 PM	(0.47) L
11:56 AM	(0.32) L	5:51 PM	(2.20) **H**	11:39 PM	(0.46) L
12:13 PM	(0.29) L	6:04 PM	(2.14) **H**	11:48 PM	(0.44) L
12:34 PM	(0.30) L	6:22 PM	(2.09) **H**		
6:29 AM	(2.70) **H**	12:59 PM	(0.36) L	6:44 PM	(2.01) **H**
6:53 AM	(2.66) **H**	1:23 PM	(0.45) L	7:05 PM	(1.93) **H**
7:15 AM	(2.58) **H**	1:44 PM	(0.55) L	7:24 PM	(1.85) **H**
7:37 AM	(2.48) **H**	2:03 PM	(0.65) L	7:41 PM	(1.77) **H**
7:58 AM	(2.34) **H**	2:26 PM	(0.78) L	7:58 PM	(1.66) **H**
8:19 AM	(2.14) **H**	2:54 PM	(0.98) L	8:09 PM	(1.48) **H**
8:35 AM	(1.85) **H**	3:45 PM	(1.26) L	6:20 PM	(1.28) **H**
10:35 AM	(1.46) L	3:25 PM	(1.60) **H**	10:13 PM	(0.91) L
10:15 AM	(1.08) L	4:08 PM	(1.91) **H**	10:25 PM	(0.68) L
10:37 AM	(0.74) L	4:40 PM	(2.13) **H**	10:44 PM	(0.53) L
11:02 AM	(0.48) L	5:06 PM	(2.22) **H**	11:00 PM	(0.49) L
11:27 AM	(0.31) L	5:29 PM	(2.22) **H**	11:15 PM	(0.49) L
11:51 AM	(0.22) L	5:49 PM	(2.14) **H**	11:29 PM	(0.51) L
12:18 PM	(0.20) L	6:10 PM	(2.03) **H**	11:44 PM	(0.54) L
12:47 PM	(0.24) L	6:33 PM	(1.89) **H**		
6:28 AM	(2.74) **H**	1:17 PM	(0.36) L	6:54 PM	(1.74) **H**
6:52 AM	(2.66) **H**	1:43 PM	(0.52) L	7:08 PM	(1.61) **H**
7:13 AM	(2.55) **H**	2:00 PM	(0.69) L	7:18 PM	(1.54) **H**

POPULAR TIDE ADJUSTMENTS

Ardossan	-6min
Brighton	-4min
Cape Jervis	- 30min
Edithburgh	- 30min
Glenelg	-10min
Port Noarlunga	-15min
Port Stanvac	-7min
Port Wakefield	- 10min
Rapid Bay	- 5min
Second Valley	-3min
Port Vincent	- 30min

Day	Date	Tide 5
Wed	4	10:00 PM (1.08) L

Adelaide Outer Harbour

Day	Date	Tide 1
Sun	1	12:33 AM (0.65) L
Mon	2	12:50 AM (0.72) L
Tue	3	1:03 AM (0.88) L
Wed	4*	12:15 AM (1.12) L
Thu	5	4:32 AM (1.66) **H**
Fri	6	4:13 AM (1.97) **H**
Sat	7	4:26 AM (2.25) **H**
Sun	8	4:44 AM (2.46) **H**
Mon	9 ●	5:02 AM (2.60) **H**
Tue	10	5:22 AM (2.69) **H**
Wed	11	5:46 AM (2.73) **H**
Thu	12	6:14 AM (2.72) **H**
Fri	13	12:12 AM (0.57) L
Sat	14	12:36 AM (0.62) L
Sun	15	1:00 AM (0.68) L
Mon	16	1:23 AM (0.76) L
Tue	17	1:52 AM (0.88) L
Wed	18	2:30 AM (1.07) L
Thu	19	4:19 AM (1.33) L
Fri	20	2:27 AM (1.69) **H**
Sat	21	3:22 AM (2.01) **H**
Sun	22	3:58 AM (2.28) **H**
Mon	23	4:28 AM (2.48) **H**
Tue	24	4:55 AM (2.63) **H**
Wed	25 ○	5:22 AM (2.72) **H**
Thu	26	5:52 AM (2.76) **H**
Fri	27	6:24 AM (2.72) **H**
Sat	28	12:12 AM (0.75) L
Sun	29	12:33 AM (0.76) L
Mon	30	12:57 AM (0.79) L

* Additional Tide 5 - See Additional Tide 5

Tide 2		Tide 3		Tide 4	
7:32 AM	(2.39) **H**	2:11 PM	(0.84) L	7:28 PM	(1.50) **H**
7:52 AM	(2.18) **H**	2:23 PM	(0.99) L	7:36 PM	(1.44) **H**
8:05 AM	(1.89) **H**	2:37 PM	(1.18) L	6:55 PM	(1.34) **H**
6:53 AM	(1.58) **H**	12:47 PM	(1.38) L	4:09 PM	(1.43) **H**
10:17 AM	(1.10) L	4:08 PM	(1.66) **H**	10:00 PM	(0.89) L
10:32 AM	(0.75) L	4:31 PM	(1.85) **H**	10:16 PM	(0.75) L
10:56 AM	(0.50) L	4:55 PM	(1.95) **H**	10:33 PM	(0.66) L
11:18 AM	(0.35) L	5:15 PM	(1.98) **H**	10:49 PM	(0.61) L
11:40 AM	(0.28) L	5:34 PM	(1.98) **H**	11:04 PM	(0.58) L
12:02 PM	(0.25) L	5:54 PM	(1.96) **H**	11:24 PM	(0.55) L
12:27 PM	(0.26) L	6:17 PM	(1.94) **H**	11:46 PM	(0.55) L
12:54 PM	(0.31) L	6:43 PM	(1.90) **H**		
6:42 AM	(2.66) **H**	1:20 PM	(0.39) L	7:09 PM	(1.85) **H**
7:08 AM	(2.56) **H**	1:45 PM	(0.48) L	7:32 PM	(1.79) **H**
7:32 AM	(2.45) **H**	2:09 PM	(0.57) L	7:55 PM	(1.74) **H**
7:58 AM	(2.32) **H**	2:36 PM	(0.67) L	8:24 PM	(1.67) **H**
8:27 AM	(2.14) **H**	3:14 PM	(0.80) L	9:09 PM	(1.57) **H**
9:09 AM	(1.90) **H**	4:22 PM	(0.97) L	11:15 PM	(1.48) **H**
11:06 AM	(1.60) **H**	7:09 PM	(1.04) L		
8:53 AM	(1.14) L	2:35 PM	(1.63) **H**	8:50 PM	(0.91) L
9:55 AM	(0.79) L	3:54 PM	(1.80) **H**	9:39 PM	(0.79) L
10:36 AM	(0.49) L	4:41 PM	(1.90) **H**	10:13 PM	(0.74) L
11:13 AM	(0.29) L	5:17 PM	(1.91) **H**	10:40 PM	(0.73) L
11:46 AM	(0.19) L	5:48 PM	(1.85) **H**	11:03 PM	(0.74) L
12:20 PM	(0.18) L	6:15 PM	(1.77) **H**	11:26 PM	(0.74) L
12:55 PM	(0.23) L	6:43 PM	(1.67) **H**	11:49 PM	(0.74) L
1:29 PM	(0.34) L	7:07 PM	(1.59) **H**		
6:54 AM	(2.62) **H**	1:58 PM	(0.49) L	7:28 PM	(1.54) **H**
7:21 AM	(2.48) **H**	2:18 PM	(0.63) L	7:46 PM	(1.55) **H**
7:46 AM	(2.31) **H**	2:32 PM	(0.73) L	8:12 PM	(1.59) **H**

Adelaide Outer Harbour

POPULAR TIDE ADJUSTMENTS

Ardossan	-6min
Brighton	-4min
Cape Jervis	- 30min
Edithburgh	- 30min
Glenelg	-10min
Port Noarlunga	-15min
Port Stanvac	-7min
Port Wakefield	- 10min
Rapid Bay	- 5min
Second Valley	-3min
Port Vincent	- 30min

Day	Date	Tide 1
Tue	1	1:29 AM (0.86) L
Wed	2	2:15 AM (1.01) L
Thu	3	3:37 AM (1.21) L
Fri	4	12:23 AM (1.71) **H**
Sat	5	2:18 AM (1.94) **H**
Sun	6	3:21 AM (2.19) **H**
Mon	7	4:05 AM (2.39) **H**
Tue	8	4:41 AM (2.53) **H**
Wed	9 ●	5:13 AM (2.61) **H**
Thu	10	5:44 AM (2.65) **H**
Fri	11	6:14 AM (2.66) **H**
Sat	12	12:17 AM (0.65) L
Sun	13	12:46 AM (0.65) L
Mon	14	1:15 AM (0.68) L
Tue	15	1:45 AM (0.74) L
Wed	16	2:22 AM (0.81) L
Thu	17	3:10 AM (0.92) L
Fri	18	4:23 AM (1.05) L
Sat	19	6:22 AM (1.11) L
Sun	20	1:22 AM (1.97) **H**
Mon	21	2:54 AM (2.15) **H**
Tue	22	3:59 AM (2.34) **H**
Wed	23	4:46 AM (2.50) **H**
Thu	24 ○	5:27 AM (2.60) **H**
Fri	25	6:02 AM (2.66) **H**
Sat	26	12:06 AM (0.82) L
Sun	27	12:37 AM (0.76) L
Mon	28	1:06 AM (0.73) L
Tue	29	1:37 AM (0.73) L
Wed	30	2:12 AM (0.76) L
Thu	31	2:53 AM (0.83) L

DECEMBER 2026

Tide 2			Tide 3			Tide 4		
8:13 AM	(2.12)	**H**	2:50 PM	(0.80)	L	8:51 PM	(1.62)	**H**
8:45 AM	(1.88)	**H**	3:20 PM	(0.88)	L	10:04 PM	(1.64)	**H**
9:36 AM	(1.59)	**H**	4:18 PM	(1.00)	L			
8:13 AM	(1.23)	L	12:35 PM	(1.34)	**H**	6:49 PM	(1.09)	L
9:50 AM	(0.92)	L	3:28 PM	(1.43)	**H**	8:41 PM	(1.02)	L
10:31 AM	(0.65)	L	4:27 PM	(1.59)	**H**	9:37 PM	(0.92)	L
11:06 AM	(0.45)	L	5:04 PM	(1.71)	**H**	10:17 PM	(0.84)	L
11:36 AM	(0.34)	L	5:35 PM	(1.79)	**H**	10:49 PM	(0.77)	L
12:04 PM	(0.28)	L	6:02 PM	(1.83)	**H**	11:19 PM	(0.72)	L
12:31 PM	(0.27)	L	6:28 PM	(1.85)	**H**	11:48 PM	(0.67)	L
12:59 PM	(0.28)	L	6:53 PM	(1.87)	**H**			
6:43 AM	(2.63)	**H**	1:25 PM	(0.32)	L	7:19 PM	(1.87)	**H**
7:11 AM	(2.57)	**H**	1:51 PM	(0.37)	L	7:45 PM	(1.86)	**H**
7:38 AM	(2.48)	**H**	2:15 PM	(0.42)	L	8:13 PM	(1.86)	**H**
8:04 AM	(2.37)	**H**	2:42 PM	(0.47)	L	8:45 PM	(1.87)	**H**
8:35 AM	(2.23)	**H**	3:12 PM	(0.54)	L	9:27 PM	(1.88)	**H**
9:15 AM	(2.03)	**H**	3:49 PM	(0.65)	L	10:23 PM	(1.88)	**H**
10:11 AM	(1.78)	**H**	4:40 PM	(0.81)	L	11:41 PM	(1.89)	**H**
11:49 AM	(1.50)	**H**	5:58 PM	(0.99)	L			
8:56 AM	(0.93)	L	2:48 PM	(1.41)	**H**	8:01 PM	(1.09)	L
10:22 AM	(0.63)	L	4:45 PM	(1.53)	**H**	9:28 PM	(1.08)	L
11:16 AM	(0.38)	L	5:39 PM	(1.62)	**H**	10:22 PM	(1.04)	L
12:00 PM	(0.23)	L	6:17 PM	(1.65)	**H**	11:02 PM	(0.97)	L
12:39 PM	(0.18)	L	6:46 PM	(1.64)	**H**	11:35 PM	(0.90)	L
1:12 PM	(0.20)	L	7:08 PM	(1.63)	**H**			
6:35 AM	(2.65)	**H**	1:40 PM	(0.28)	L	7:28 PM	(1.64)	**H**
7:05 AM	(2.57)	**H**	2:02 PM	(0.38)	L	7:45 PM	(1.70)	**H**
7:32 AM	(2.45)	**H**	2:17 PM	(0.47)	L	8:05 PM	(1.79)	**H**
7:56 AM	(2.30)	**H**	2:27 PM	(0.51)	L	8:30 PM	(1.92)	**H**
8:19 AM	(2.15)	**H**	2:40 PM	(0.51)	L	9:00 PM	(2.04)	**H**
8:45 AM	(1.98)	**H**	2:59 PM	(0.51)	L	9:42 PM	(2.10)	**H**

Apogee moon phase on Friday 24th
Perigee moon phase on Wednesday 8th
● New moon on Tuesday 21st
First quarter moon on Thursday 30th
○ Full moon on Tuesday 7th
Last quarter moon phase on Tuesday 14th

Adelaide, SA: Rise: 06:30am Set: 07:20pm

Note: Daylight Savings start (clocks turn forward 1 hour) on Sunday, October 2nd at 2:00 AM. Subtract 1 hour to rise/set time for days before October 2nd. These sun rise/set times are averages for the mont

DAY	MINOR BITE	MAJOR BITE	MINOR BITE	MAJOR BITE	SALT WATER RATING	FRESH WATE RATING
WED 1	10:42 AM	6:28 PM	1:24 AM	6:01 AM	5	6
THUR 2	11:48 AM	7:19 PM	2:05 AM	6:53 AM	4	5
FRI 3	12:57 PM	8:09 PM	2:40 AM	7:44 AM	3	5
SAT 4	2:07 PM	8:58 PM	3:10 AM	8:33 AM	6	6
SUN 5	3:17 PM	9:47 PM	3:38 AM	9:22 AM	5	7
MON 6	4:30 PM	10:36 PM	4:04 AM	10:11 AM	3	8
TUE 7	5:44 PM	11:27 PM	4:30 AM	11:01 AM	○ 5	7
WED 8	7:01 PM		4:59 AM	11:54 AM	7	6
THUR 9	8:21 PM	12:21 AM	5:31 AM	12:50 PM	7	6
FRI 10	9:39 PM	1:19 AM	6:10 AM	1:50 PM	5	5
SAT 11	10:53 PM	2:21 AM	6:58 AM	2:52 PM	4	4

OCTOBER 2025

POPULAR LOCATION ADJUSTMENTS (See full list on page 7)

DAY	MINOR BITE	MAJOR BITE	MINOR BITE	MAJOR BITE	SALT WATER RATING	FRESH WATER RATING
SUN 12	11:57 PM	3:25 AM	7:55 AM	3:56 PM	3	6
MON 13		4:28 AM	9:01 AM	4:57 PM	4	4
TUE 14	12:48 AM	5:27 AM	10:11 AM	5:54 PM	5	5
WED 15	1:30 AM	6:22 AM	11:21 AM	6:47 PM	6	6
THUR 16	2:03 AM	7:12 AM	12:29 PM	7:34 PM	7	7
FRI 17	2:30 AM	7:58 AM	1:34 PM	8:18 PM	7	8
SAT 18	2:54 AM	8:40 AM	2:35 PM	9:00 PM	5	8
SUN 19	3:16 AM	9:21 AM	3:36 PM	9:41 PM	6	7
MON 20	3:37 AM	10:01 AM	4:35 PM	10:21 PM	8	8
TUE 21	3:59 AM	10:42 AM	5:35 PM	11:03 PM	● 8	8
WED 22	4:23 AM	11:24 AM	6:35 PM	11:45 PM	8	8
THUR 23	4:49 AM	12:08 PM	7:36 PM		8	6
FRI 24	5:20 AM	12:55 PM	8:37 PM	12:31 AM	7	6
SAT 25	5:57 AM	1:44 PM	9:36 PM	1:19 AM	6	7
SUN 26	6:41 AM	2:35 PM	10:31 PM	2:09 AM	5	5
MON 27	7:32 AM	3:27 PM	11:19 PM	3:00 AM	4	6
TUE 28	8:30 AM	4:19 PM		3:53 AM	3	5
WED 29	9:33 AM	5:10 PM	12:01 AM	4:44 AM	3	5
THUR 30	10:39 AM	5:59 PM	12:37 AM	5:34 AM	4	6
FRI 31	11:46 AM	6:47 PM	1:08 AM	6:23 AM	5	6

Apogee moon phase on Thursday 20th
Perigee moon phase on Thursday 6th
● New moon on Thursday 20th
First quarter moon on Friday 28th
○ Full moon on Thursday 6th
Last quarter moon phase on Wednesday 12th

Adelaide, SA: Rise: 06:00am Set: 07:50pm
(Note: These sun rise/set times are averages for the month)

DAY	MINOR BITE	MAJOR BITE	MINOR BITE	MAJOR BITE	SALT WATER RATING	FRESH WATER RATING
SAT 1	12:54 PM	7:34 PM	1:36 AM	7:10 AM	4	5
SUN 2	2:04 PM	8:21 PM	2:02 AM	7:57 AM	3	5
MON 3	3:16 PM	9:11 PM	2:28 AM	8:46 AM	6	6
TUE 4	4:31 PM	10:03 PM	2:55 AM	9:37 AM	3	8
WED 5	5:50 PM	11:00 PM	3:25 AM	10:31 AM	5	7
THUR 6	7:12 PM		4:01 AM	11:31 AM	○ 7	6
FRI 7	8:31 PM	12:02 AM	4:46 AM	12:34 PM	7	6
SAT 8	9:42 PM	1:07 AM	5:41 AM	1:39 PM	5	5
SUN 9	10:41 PM	2:13 AM	6:46 AM	2:45 PM	4	4
MON 10	11:27 PM	3:17 AM	7:57 AM	3:46 PM	3	6
TUE 11		4:16 AM	9:10 AM	4:41 PM	4	4

NOVEMBER 2025

POPULAR LOCATION ADJUSTMENTS (See full list on page 7)

DAY	MINOR BITE	MAJOR BITE	MINOR BITE	MAJOR BITE	SALT WATER RATING	FRESH WATER RATING
WED 12	12:04 AM	5:08 AM	10:20 AM	5:32 PM	5	5
THUR 13	12:33 AM	5:56 AM	11:27 AM	6:18 PM	6	6
FRI 14	12:59 AM	6:40 AM	12:29 PM	7:00 PM	7	7
SAT 15	1:21 AM	7:21 AM	1:30 PM	7:41 PM	7	7
SUN 16	1:42 AM	8:01 AM	2:29 PM	8:21 PM	7	8
MON 17	2:04 AM	8:41 AM	3:28 PM	9:01 PM	5	8
TUE 18	2:27 AM	9:22 AM	4:28 PM	9:44 PM	6	7
WED 19	2:53 AM	10:06 AM	5:29 PM	10:29 PM	8	8
THUR 20	3:22 AM	10:52 AM	6:30 PM	11:15 PM	● 8	8
FRI 21	3:57 AM	11:40 AM	7:29 PM		8	6
SAT 22	4:39 AM	12:31 PM	8:25 PM	12:05 AM	7	6
SUN 23	5:28 AM	1:23 PM	9:16 PM	12:57 AM	7	6
MON 24	6:24 AM	2:15 PM	10:00 PM	1:49 AM	6	7
TUE 25	7:25 AM	3:05 PM	10:37 PM	2:39 AM	5	5
WED 26	8:29 AM	3:54 PM	11:09 PM	3:29 AM	4	6
THUR 27	9:34 AM	4:41 PM	11:37 PM	4:17 AM	3	5
FRI 28	10:39 AM	5:26 PM		5:03 AM	4	6
SAT 29	11:46 AM	6:12 PM	12:02 AM	5:48 AM	5	6
SUN 30	12:54 PM	6:58 PM	12:27 AM	6:34 AM	4	5

Apogee moon phase on Wednesday 17th
Perigee moon phase on Thursday 4th
● New moon on Saturday 20th
First quarter moon on Sunday 28th
○ Full moon on Friday 5th
Last quarter moon phase on Friday 12th

Adelaide, SA: Rise: 05:50am Set: 08:20pm
(Note: These sun rise/set times are averages for the month)

DAY	MINOR BITE	MAJOR BITE	MINOR BITE	MAJOR BITE	SALT WATER RATING	FRESH WATER RATING
MON 1	2:04 PM	7:47 PM	12:52 AM	7:22 AM	3	5
TUE 2	3:19 PM	8:40 PM	1:20 AM	8:13 AM	6	6
WED 3	4:38 PM	9:39 PM	1:52 AM	9:09 AM	5	7
THUR 4	5:59 PM	10:43 PM	2:31 AM	10:11 AM	3	8
FRI 5	7:16 PM	11:50 PM	3:21 AM	11:16 AM	○ 5	7
SAT 6	8:23 PM		4:22 AM	12:23 PM	7	6
SUN 7	9:17 PM	12:57 AM	5:33 AM	1:28 PM	7	6
MON 8	10:00 PM	2:00 AM	6:49 AM	2:28 PM	5	5
TUE 9	10:33 PM	2:58 AM	8:03 AM	3:23 PM	4	4
WED 10	11:01 PM	3:49 AM	9:13 AM	4:12 PM	3	6
THUR 11	11:25 PM	4:36 AM	10:19 AM	4:57 PM	4	4

DECEMBER 2025

POPULAR LOCATION ADJUSTMENTS (See full list on page 7)

DAY	MINOR BITE	MAJOR BITE	MINOR BITE	MAJOR BITE	SALT WATER RATING	FRESH WATER RATING
RI 12	11:47 PM	5:19 AM	11:22 AM	5:39 PM	5	5
AT 13		6:00 AM	12:22 PM	6:19 PM	6	6
UN 14	12:08 AM	6:40 AM	1:21 PM	7:00 PM	7	7
ION 15	12:31 AM	7:21 AM	2:21 PM	7:42 PM	7	8
UE 16	12:56 AM	8:04 AM	3:21 PM	8:26 PM	5	8
VED 17	1:24 AM	8:49 AM	4:22 PM	9:12 PM	5	8
HUR 18	1:57 AM	9:36 AM	5:22 PM	10:01 PM	6	7
RI 19	2:37 AM	10:27 AM	6:20 PM	10:52 PM	8	8
AT 20	3:24 AM	11:19 AM	7:13 PM	11:45 PM	● 8	8
UN 21	4:19 AM	12:11 PM	7:59 PM		8	6
ION 22	5:19 AM	1:02 PM	8:38 PM	12:36 AM	7	6
UE 23	6:22 AM	1:52 PM	9:11 PM	1:26 AM	6	7
VED 24	7:27 AM	2:39 PM	9:40 PM	2:15 AM	5	5
HUR 25	8:32 AM	3:24 PM	10:06 PM	3:01 AM	4	6
RI 26	9:37 AM	4:09 PM	10:30 PM	3:46 AM	4	6
AT 27	10:42 AM	4:53 PM	10:54 PM	4:30 AM	3	5
UN 28	11:49 AM	5:39 PM	11:19 PM	5:15 AM	4	6
ION 29	12:59 PM	6:28 PM	11:48 PM	6:03 AM	5	6
UE 30	2:14 PM	7:22 PM		6:55 AM	4	5
VED 31	3:31 PM	8:21 PM	12:23 AM	7:51 AM	3	5

Apogee moon phase on Wednesday 14th
Perigee moon phase on Friday 2nd and Friday 30th
● New moon on Monday 19th
First quarter moon on Monday 26th
○ Full moon on Saturday 3rd
Last quarter moon phase on Sunday 11th

Adelaide, SA: Rise: 05:50am Set: 08:20pm
(Note: These sun rise/set times are averages for the month)

DAY	MINOR BITE	MAJOR BITE	MINOR BITE	MAJOR BITE	SALT WATER RATING	FRESH WATE RATING
THUR 1	4:48 PM	9:26 PM	1:06 AM	8:53 AM	5	7
FRI 2	6:00 PM	10:32 PM	2:00 AM	9:58 AM	3	8
SAT 3	7:01 PM	11:38 PM	3:06 AM	11:05 AM	○ 5	7
SUN 4	7:50 PM		4:20 AM	12:09 PM	7	6
MON 5	8:28 PM	12:40 AM	5:37 AM	1:07 PM	7	6
TUE 6	8:59 PM	1:35 AM	6:51 AM	2:00 PM	5	5
WED 7	9:25 PM	2:26 AM	8:01 AM	2:48 PM	4	4
THUR 8	9:49 PM	3:11 AM	9:07 AM	3:32 PM	3	6
FRI 9	10:11 PM	3:54 AM	10:10 AM	4:15 PM	3	6
SAT 10	10:33 PM	4:36 AM	11:11 AM	4:56 PM	4	4
SUN 11	10:57 PM	5:17 AM	12:12 PM	5:38 PM	5	5

JANUARY 2026

POPULAR LOCATION ADJUSTMENTS (See full list on page 7)

DAY	MINOR BITE	MAJOR BITE	MINOR BITE	MAJOR BITE	SALT WATER RATING	FRESH WATER RATING
ION 12	11:24 PM	6:00 AM	1:12 PM	6:22 PM	6	6
UE 13	11:56 PM	6:44 AM	2:13 PM	7:07 PM	7	7
VED 14		7:31 AM	3:14 PM	7:55 PM	7	8
HUR 15	12:33 AM	8:20 AM	4:12 PM	8:45 PM	5	8
RI 16	1:18 AM	9:12 AM	5:07 PM	9:38 PM	6	7
AT 17	2:10 AM	10:05 AM	5:55 PM	10:30 PM	8	8
UN 18	3:09 AM	10:57 AM	6:37 PM	11:22 PM	8	8
ION 19	4:13 AM	11:48 AM	7:13 PM		● 8	8
UE 20	5:18 AM	12:36 PM	7:43 PM	12:12 AM	8	6
VED 21	6:24 AM	1:23 PM	8:10 PM	12:59 AM	7	6
HUR 22	7:30 AM	2:08 PM	8:35 PM	1:45 AM	6	7
RI 23	8:35 AM	2:52 PM	8:58 PM	2:30 AM	5	5
AT 24	9:41 AM	3:37 PM	9:23 PM	3:14 AM	4	6
UN 25	10:50 AM	4:24 PM	9:50 PM	4:00 AM	3	5
ION 26	12:01 PM	5:15 PM	10:21 PM	4:49 AM	4	6
UE 27	1:15 PM	6:10 PM	10:59 PM	5:42 AM	5	6
VED 28	2:30 PM	7:10 PM	11:47 PM	6:40 AM	4	5
HUR 29	3:42 PM	8:14 PM		7:42 AM	3	5
RI 30	4:46 PM	9:19 PM	12:46 AM	8:46 AM	6	6
AT 31	5:39 PM	10:21 PM	1:55 AM	9:50 AM	5	7

Apogee moon phase on Wednesday 11th
Perigee moon phase on Wednesday 25th
● New moon on Tuesday 17th
First quarter moon on Tuesday 24th
○ Full moon on Monday 2nd
Last quarter moon phase on Monday 9th

Adelaide, SA: Rise: 06:40am Set: 08:10pm
(Note: These sun rise/set times are averages for the month)

DAY	MINOR BITE	MAJOR BITE	MINOR BITE	MAJOR BITE	SALT WATER RATING	FRESH WATE RATING
SUN 1	6:21 PM	11:19 PM	3:10 AM	10:50 AM	3	8
MON 2	6:55 PM		4:25 AM	11:45 AM	○ 5	7
TUE 3	7:24 PM	12:12 AM	5:38 AM	12:36 PM	7	6
WED 4	7:49 PM	1:01 AM	6:47 AM	1:23 PM	7	6
THUR 5	8:12 PM	1:46 AM	7:53 AM	2:07 PM	5	5
FRI 6	8:35 PM	2:29 AM	8:56 AM	2:50 PM	4	4
SAT 7	8:58 PM	3:11 AM	9:58 AM	3:32 PM	3	6
SUN 8	9:24 PM	3:54 AM	10:59 AM	4:15 PM	4	4
MON 9	9:54 PM	4:38 AM	12:01 PM	5:00 PM	5	5
TUE 10	10:29 PM	5:24 AM	1:02 PM	5:48 PM	5	5
WED 11	11:11 PM	6:12 AM	2:02 PM	6:37 PM	6	6

FEBRUARY 2026

POPULAR LOCATION ADJUSTMENTS (See full list on page 7)

DAY	MINOR BITE	MAJOR BITE	MINOR BITE	MAJOR BITE	SALT WATER RATING	FRESH WATER RATING
HUR 12		7:03 AM	2:58 PM	7:29 PM	7	7
RI 13		7:55 AM	3:49 PM	8:21 PM	7	8
AT 14	12:56 AM	8:48 AM	4:33 PM	9:13 PM	5	8
UN 15	1:59 AM	9:39 AM	5:11 PM	10:03 PM	6	7
ION 16	3:04 AM	10:29 AM	5:44 PM	10:52 PM	8	8
UE 17	4:11 AM	11:17 AM	6:12 PM	11:40 PM	● 8	8
VED 18	5:18 AM	12:03 PM	6:38 PM		8	6
HUR 19	6:25 AM	12:49 PM	7:02 PM	12:26 AM	7	6
RI 20	7:32 AM	1:35 PM	7:27 PM	1:11 AM	6	7
AT 21	8:41 AM	2:22 PM	7:54 PM	1:58 AM	5	5
UN 22	9:52 AM	3:12 PM	8:24 PM	2:46 AM	4	6
ION 23	11:05 AM	4:06 PM	8:59 PM	3:38 AM	3	5
UE 24	12:20 PM	5:04 PM	9:43 PM	4:34 AM	4	6
VED 25	1:32 PM	6:05 PM	10:37 PM	5:34 AM	5	6
HUR 26	2:37 PM	7:08 PM	11:41 PM	6:36 AM	4	5
RI 27	3:32 PM	8:10 PM		7:39 AM	3	5
AT 28	4:17 PM	9:08 PM	12:52 AM	8:39 AM	6	6

Apogee moon phase on Tuesday 10th
Perigee moon phase on Sunday 22nd
● New moon on Thursday 19th
First quarter moon on Thursday 26th
○ Full moon on Tuesday 3rd
Last quarter moon phase on Wednesday 11th

Adelaide, SA: Rise: 07:10am Set: 07:30pm
(Note: These sun rise/set times are averages for the month)

DAY	MINOR BITE	MAJOR BITE	MINOR BITE	MAJOR BITE	SALT WATER RATING	FRESH WATER RATING
SUN 1	4:53 PM	10:02 PM	2:06 AM	9:35 AM	5	7
MON 2	5:23 PM	10:51 PM	3:18 AM	10:26 AM	3	8
TUE 3	5:49 PM	11:37 PM	4:28 AM	11:13 AM	○ 5	7
WED 4	6:13 PM		5:34 AM	11:58 AM	7	6
THUR 5	6:36 PM	12:21 AM	6:39 AM	12:42 PM	7	6
FRI 6	6:59 PM	1:04 AM	7:42 AM	1:24 PM	7	6
SAT 7	7:25 PM	1:46 AM	8:44 AM	2:07 PM	5	5
SUN 8	7:53 PM	2:30 AM	9:46 AM	2:52 PM	4	4
MON 9	8:26 PM	3:16 AM	10:49 AM	3:39 PM	3	6
TUE 10	9:05 PM	4:04 AM	11:50 AM	4:29 PM	4	4
WED 11	9:51 PM	4:54 AM	12:47 PM	5:19 PM	5	5

MARCH 2026

POPULAR LOCATION ADJUSTMENTS (See full list on page 7)

DAY	MINOR BITE	MAJOR BITE	MINOR BITE	MAJOR BITE	SALT WATER RATING	FRESH WATER RATING
UR 12	10:44 PM	5:45 AM	1:40 PM	6:11 PM	6	6
I 13	11:43 PM	6:37 AM	2:27 PM	7:03 PM	7	7
T 14		7:29 AM	3:07 PM	7:53 PM	7	7
N 15	12:47 AM	8:19 AM	3:42 PM	8:43 PM	7	8
ON 16	1:52 AM	9:08 AM	4:12 PM	9:31 PM	5	8
E 17	2:59 AM	9:55 AM	4:39 PM	10:18 PM	6	7
ED 18	4:07 AM	10:41 AM	5:04 PM	11:03 PM	8	8
HUR 19	5:15 AM	11:27 AM	5:29 PM	11:51 PM	● 8	8
I 20	6:25 AM	12:15 PM	5:55 PM		8	6
AT 21	7:37 AM	1:06 PM	6:25 PM	12:40 AM	7	6
UN 22	8:52 AM	2:00 PM	6:59 PM	1:33 AM	6	7
ON 23	10:08 AM	2:58 PM	7:41 PM	2:29 AM	5	5
UE 24	11:23 AM	3:59 PM	8:33 PM	3:28 AM	4	6
ED 25	12:31 PM	5:02 PM	9:34 PM	4:30 AM	3	5
HUR 26	1:29 PM	6:04 PM	10:43 PM	5:32 AM	4	6
RI 27	2:16 PM	7:03 PM	11:55 PM	6:33 AM	5	6
AT 28	2:54 PM	7:57 PM		7:30 AM	4	5
UN 29	3:26 PM	8:46 PM	1:06 AM	8:21 AM	3	5
ON 30	3:52 PM	9:32 PM	2:15 AM	9:09 AM	6	6
UE 31	4:16 PM	10:16 PM	3:21 AM	9:54 AM	5	7

Apogee moon phase on Tuesday 7th
Perigee moon phase on Sunday 19th
● New moon on Friday 17th
First quarter moon on Friday 24th
○ Full moon on Thursday 2nd
Last quarter moon phase on Friday 10th

Adelaide, SA: Rise: 06:30am Set: 05:50pm

Note: Daylight Savings ends (clocks turn backward 1 hour) on Sunday, 6th April at 3:00 AM. Add 1 hour to rise/set time for days before April 7th. These sun rise/set times are averages for the month

DAY	MINOR BITE	MAJOR BITE	MINOR BITE	MAJOR BITE	SALT WATER RATING	FRESH WAT RATING
WED 1	4:39 PM	10:58 PM	4:26 AM	10:37 AM	3	8
THUR 2	5:02 PM	11:41 PM	5:28 AM	11:19 AM	○ 5	7
FRI 3	5:26 PM		6:30 AM	12:02 PM	7	6
SAT 4	5:53 PM	12:24 AM	7:33 AM	12:46 PM	7	6
SUN 5	6:25 PM	1:09 AM	8:35 AM	1:33 PM	5	5
MON 6	7:01 PM	1:57 AM	9:37 AM	2:21 PM	5	5
TUE 7	7:44 PM	2:46 AM	10:36 AM	3:11 PM	4	4
WED 8	8:34 PM	3:37 AM	11:31 AM	4:02 PM	3	6
THUR 9	9:30 PM	4:28 AM	12:20 PM	4:53 PM	4	4
FRI 10	10:31 PM	5:20 AM	1:03 PM	5:44 PM	5	5
SAT 11	11:35 PM	6:09 AM	1:39 PM	6:33 PM	6	6

APRIL 2026

POPULAR LOCATION ADJUSTMENTS (See full list on page 7)

DAY	MINOR BITE	MAJOR BITE	MINOR BITE	MAJOR BITE	SALT WATER RATING	FRESH WATER RATING
N 12		6:58 AM	2:10 PM	7:21 PM	7	7
ON 13	12:40 AM	7:44 AM	2:38 PM	8:07 PM	7	8
E 14	1:46 AM	8:30 AM	3:03 PM	8:52 PM	5	8
ED 15	2:53 AM	9:16 AM	3:28 PM	9:39 PM	6	7
UR 16	4:02 AM	10:03 AM	3:54 PM	10:27 PM	8	8
I 17	5:14 AM	10:53 AM	4:22 PM	11:19 PM	● 8	8
T 18	6:29 AM	11:47 AM	4:55 PM		8	6
N 19	7:47 AM	12:45 PM	5:35 PM	12:16 AM	7	6
ON 20	9:06 AM	1:47 PM	6:25 PM	1:15 AM	6	7
E 21	10:19 AM	2:52 PM	7:24 PM	2:19 AM	5	5
ED 22	11:23 AM	3:56 PM	8:33 PM	3:23 AM	4	6
UR 23	12:14 PM	4:57 PM	9:46 PM	4:26 AM	3	5
I 24	12:56 PM	5:53 PM	10:58 PM	5:25 AM	4	6
T 25	1:29 PM	6:44 PM		6:18 AM	5	6
N 26	1:56 PM	7:31 PM	12:08 AM	7:07 AM	4	5
ON 27	2:21 PM	8:14 PM	1:14 AM	7:52 AM	3	5
E 28	2:44 PM	8:57 PM	2:18 AM	8:35 AM	6	6
ED 29	3:06 PM	9:38 PM	3:20 AM	9:17 AM	5	7
UR 30	3:30 PM	10:21 PM	4:21 AM	9:59 AM	5	7

Apogee moon phase on Tuesday 5th
Perigee moon phase on Sunday 17th
● New moon on Sunday 17th
First quarter moon on Saturday 23rd
○ Full moon on Saturday 2nd and Sunday 31st
Last quarter moon phase on Sunday 10th

Adelaide, SA: Rise: 07:00am Set: 05:20pm

(Note: These sun rise/set times are averages for the month)

DAY	MINOR BITE	MAJOR BITE	MINOR BITE	MAJOR BITE	SALT WATER RATING	FRESH WAT RATING
FRI 1	3:56 PM	11:05 PM	5:23 AM	10:43 AM	3	8
SAT 2	4:25 PM	11:52 PM	6:25 AM	11:28 AM	○ 5	7
SUN 3	5:00 PM		7:27 AM	12:16 PM	7	6
MON 4	5:41 PM	12:40 AM	8:27 AM	1:05 PM	7	6
TUE 5	6:28 PM	1:31 AM	9:24 AM	1:56 PM	5	5
WED 6	7:22 PM	2:22 AM	10:15 AM	2:47 PM	4	4
THUR 7	8:21 PM	3:13 AM	10:59 AM	3:37 PM	3	6
FRI 8	9:23 PM	4:03 AM	11:37 AM	4:26 PM	3	6
SAT 9	10:26 PM	4:51 AM	12:09 PM	5:14 PM	4	4
SUN 10	11:30 PM	5:37 AM	12:38 PM	5:59 PM	5	5
MON 11		6:22 AM	1:03 PM	6:44 PM	6	6

MAY 2026

POPULAR LOCATION ADJUSTMENTS (See full list on page 7)

DAY	MINOR BITE	MAJOR BITE	MINOR BITE	MAJOR BITE	SALT WATER RATING	FRESH WATER RATING
UE 12	12:34 AM	7:06 AM	1:28 PM	7:29 PM	7	7
VED 13	1:41 AM	7:52 AM	1:52 PM	8:15 PM	7	8
HUR 14	2:49 AM	8:39 AM	2:19 PM	9:04 PM	5	8
RI 15	4:02 AM	9:30 AM	2:49 PM	9:57 PM	6	7
AT 16	5:19 AM	10:26 AM	3:26 PM	10:56 PM	8	8
UN 17	6:39 AM	11:28 AM	4:11 PM		● 8	8
ON 18	7:57 AM	12:33 PM	5:08 PM	12:00 AM	8	6
UE 19	9:07 AM	1:41 PM	6:16 PM	1:07 AM	7	6
VED 20	10:06 AM	2:46 PM	7:30 PM	2:13 AM	6	7
HUR 21	10:53 AM	3:46 PM	8:45 PM	3:15 AM	5	5
RI 22	11:30 AM	4:40 PM	9:58 PM	4:13 AM	3	5
AT 23	12:00 PM	5:28 PM	11:06 PM	5:03 AM	4	6
UN 24	12:25 PM	6:13 PM		5:50 AM	5	6
ON 25	12:49 PM	6:56 PM	12:11 AM	6:34 AM	5	6
UE 26	1:11 PM	7:38 PM	1:14 AM	7:16 AM	4	5
VED 27	1:34 PM	8:20 PM	2:15 AM	7:59 AM	3	5
HUR 28	1:59 PM	9:03 PM	3:16 AM	8:41 AM	6	6
RI 29	2:28 PM	9:49 PM	4:17 AM	9:26 AM	5	7
AT 30	3:00 PM	10:36 PM	5:19 AM	10:12 AM	3	8
UN 31	3:39 PM	11:26 PM	6:20 AM	11:01 AM	○ 5	7

Apogee moon phase on Monday 1st and Sunday 28th

Perigee moon phase on Monday 15th

● New moon on Monday 15th

First quarter moon on Monday 22nd

○ Full moon on Tuesday 30th

Last quarter moon phase on Monday 8th

Adelaide, SA: Rise: 07:20am Set: 05:10pm

(Note: These sun rise/set times are averages for the month)

DAY	MINOR BITE	MAJOR BITE	MINOR BITE	MAJOR BITE	SALT WATER RATING	FRESH WATER RATING
MON 1	4:25 PM		7:17 AM	11:51 AM	7	6
TUE 2	5:17 PM	12:17 AM	8:10 AM	12:43 PM	7	6
WED 3	6:14 PM	1:09 AM	8:57 AM	1:33 PM	7	6
THUR 4	7:15 PM	1:59 AM	9:36 AM	2:22 PM	5	5
FRI 5	8:17 PM	2:47 AM	10:10 AM	3:09 PM	4	4
SAT 6	9:20 PM	3:33 AM	10:39 AM	3:55 PM	3	6
SUN 7	10:22 PM	4:18 AM	11:05 AM	4:39 PM	4	4
MON 8	11:26 PM	5:01 AM	11:29 AM	5:22 PM	5	5
TUE 9		5:44 AM	11:53 AM	6:06 PM	6	6
WED 10	12:31 AM	6:29 AM	12:18 PM	6:52 PM	7	7
THUR 11	1:40 AM	7:17 AM	12:45 PM	7:42 PM	7	8

JUNE 2026

POPULAR LOCATION ADJUSTMENTS (See full list on page 7)

DAY	MINOR BITE	MAJOR BITE	MINOR BITE	MAJOR BITE	SALT WATER RATING	FRESH WATER RATING
RI 12	2:52 AM	8:09 AM	1:18 PM	8:37 PM	5	8
AT 13	4:09 AM	9:07 AM	1:58 PM	9:38 PM	6	7
UN 14	5:28 AM	10:10 AM	2:49 PM	10:44 PM	8	8
ON 15	6:44 AM	11:18 AM	3:52 PM	11:52 PM	● 8	8
UE 16	7:49 AM	12:26 PM	5:05 PM		8	6
ED 17	8:43 AM	1:30 PM	6:23 PM	12:58 AM	7	6
HUR 18	9:25 AM	2:28 PM	7:40 PM	1:59 AM	6	7
RI 19	9:59 AM	3:21 PM	8:52 PM	2:54 AM	5	5
AT 20	10:27 AM	4:09 PM	10:00 PM	3:45 AM	4	6
UN 21	10:52 AM	4:54 PM	11:05 PM	4:31 AM	3	5
ON 22	11:15 AM	5:36 PM		5:15 AM	4	6
UE 23	11:38 AM	6:19 PM	12:08 AM	5:57 AM	5	6
ED 24	12:03 PM	7:02 PM	1:09 AM	6:40 AM	4	5
HUR 25	12:30 PM	7:46 PM	2:11 AM	7:24 AM	3	5
RI 26	1:01 PM	8:33 PM	3:12 AM	8:09 AM	6	6
AT 27	1:38 PM	9:22 PM	4:13 AM	8:57 AM	6	6
UN 28	2:21 PM	10:13 PM	5:12 AM	9:47 AM	5	7
ON 29	3:12 PM	11:05 PM	6:06 AM	10:39 AM	3	8
UE 30	4:08 PM	11:55 PM	6:55 AM	11:30 AM	○ 5	7

Apogee moon phase on Sunday 26th
Perigee moon phase on Monday 13th
● **New moon on Tuesday 14th**
First quarter moon on Tuesday 21st
○ **Full moon on Thursday 30th**
Last quarter moon phase on Wednesday 8th

Adelaide, SA: Rise: 07:20am Set: 05:20pm
(Note: These sun rise/set times are averages for the month)

DAY	MINOR BITE	MAJOR BITE	MINOR BITE	MAJOR BITE	SALT WATER RATING	FRESH WATER RATING
WED 1	5:09 PM		7:36 AM	12:20 PM	7	6
THUR 2	6:10 PM	12:45 AM	8:12 AM	1:07 PM	7	6
FRI 3	7:13 PM	1:31 AM	8:42 AM	1:53 PM	5	5
SAT 4	8:15 PM	2:16 AM	9:09 AM	2:37 PM	4	4
SUN 5	9:18 PM	2:59 AM	9:33 AM	3:20 PM	3	6
MON 6	10:21 PM	3:42 AM	9:56 AM	4:03 PM	3	6
TUE 7	11:26 PM	4:25 AM	10:20 AM	4:48 PM	4	4
WED 8		5:11 AM	10:45 AM	5:34 PM	5	5
THUR 9	12:35 AM	5:59 AM	11:15 AM	6:26 PM	6	6
FRI 10	1:48 AM	6:53 AM	11:50 AM	7:22 PM	7	7
SAT 11	3:04 AM	7:52 AM	12:34 PM	8:23 PM	7	8

POPULAR LOCATION ADJUSTMENTS (See full list on page 7)

DAY	MINOR BITE	MAJOR BITE	MINOR BITE	MAJOR BITE	SALT WATER RATING	FRESH WATER RATING
SUN 12	4:19 AM	8:56 AM	1:30 PM	9:29 PM	6	7
MON 13	5:29 AM	10:03 AM	2:38 PM	10:36 PM	8	8
TUE 14	6:29 AM	11:09 AM	3:54 PM	11:40 PM	● 8	8
WED 15	7:16 AM	12:11 PM	5:13 PM		8	6
THUR 16	7:54 AM	1:08 PM	6:30 PM	12:39 AM	7	6
FRI 17	8:26 AM	1:59 PM	7:42 PM	1:33 AM	6	7
SAT 18	8:52 AM	2:46 PM	8:50 PM	2:22 AM	5	5
SUN 19	9:17 AM	3:31 PM	9:55 PM	3:08 AM	4	6
MON 20	9:41 AM	4:14 PM	10:59 PM	3:52 AM	3	5
TUE 21	10:05 AM	4:58 PM		4:35 AM	4	6
WED 22	10:32 AM	5:43 PM	12:01 AM	5:20 AM	5	6
THUR 23	11:02 AM	6:29 PM	1:04 AM	6:05 AM	5	6
FRI 24	11:37 AM	7:18 PM	2:05 AM	6:53 AM	4	5
SAT 25	12:18 PM	8:08 PM	3:05 AM	7:43 AM	3	5
SUN 26	1:06 PM	8:59 PM	4:01 AM	8:33 AM	6	6
MON 27	2:00 PM	9:51 PM	4:52 AM	9:24 AM	5	7
TUE 28	3:00 PM	10:41 PM	5:36 AM	10:16 AM	3	8
WED 29	4:02 PM	11:29 PM	6:13 AM	11:05 AM	5	7
THUR 30	5:05 PM		6:45 AM	11:52 AM	○ 5	7
FRI 31	6:09 PM	12:15 AM	7:13 AM	12:37 PM	7	6

Apogee moon phase on Saturday 22nd
Perigee moon phase on Monday 10th
● New moon on Thursday 13th
First quarter moon on Thursday 20th
○ Full moon on Friday 28th
Last quarter moon phase on Thursday 6th

Adelaide, SA: Rise: 06:50am Set: 05:40pm
(Note: These sun rise/set times are averages for the month)

DAY	MINOR BITE	MAJOR BITE	MINOR BITE	MAJOR BITE	SALT WATER RATING	FRESH WATER RATING
SAT 1	7:12 PM	12:59 AM	7:38 AM	1:20 PM	7	6
SUN 2	8:14 PM	1:42 AM	8:02 AM	2:03 PM	5	5
MON 3	9:19 PM	2:25 AM	8:25 AM	2:46 PM	4	4
TUE 4	10:26 PM	3:09 AM	8:49 AM	3:31 PM	3	6
WED 5	11:35 PM	3:55 AM	9:17 AM	4:20 PM	4	4
THUR 6		4:46 AM	9:49 AM	5:13 PM	5	5
FRI 7	12:48 AM	5:41 AM	10:28 AM	6:11 PM	6	6
SAT 8	2:02 AM	6:41 AM	11:17 AM	7:12 PM	7	7
SUN 9	3:12 AM	7:45 AM	12:18 PM	8:17 PM	7	8
MON 10	4:15 AM	8:50 AM	1:29 PM	9:21 PM	5	8
TUE 11	5:07 AM	9:53 AM	2:46 PM	10:22 PM	6	7

AUGUST 2026

POPULAR LOCATION ADJUSTMENTS (See full list on page 7)

DAY	MINOR BITE	MAJOR BITE	MINOR BITE	MAJOR BITE	SALT WATER RATING	FRESH WATER RATING
WED 12	5:48 AM	10:52 AM	4:04 PM	11:18 PM	8	8
THUR 13	6:22 AM	11:46 AM	5:18 PM		● 8	8
FRI 14	6:51 AM	12:35 PM	6:29 PM	12:10 AM	8	6
SAT 15	7:17 AM	1:22 PM	7:37 PM	12:58 AM	7	6
SUN 16	7:41 AM	2:07 PM	8:43 PM	1:44 AM	6	7
MON 17	8:06 AM	2:51 PM	9:47 PM	2:29 AM	5	5
TUE 18	8:32 AM	3:36 PM	10:51 PM	3:13 AM	4	6
WED 19	9:01 AM	4:23 PM	11:54 PM	3:59 AM	3	5
THUR 20	9:34 AM	5:11 PM		4:46 AM	4	6
FRI 21	10:13 AM	6:01 PM	12:55 AM	5:35 AM	5	6
SAT 22	10:59 AM	6:52 PM	1:53 AM	6:26 AM	4	5
SUN 23	11:51 AM	7:44 PM	2:46 AM	7:17 AM	3	5
MON 24	12:49 PM	8:34 PM	3:32 AM	8:09 AM	3	5
TUE 25	1:51 PM	9:23 PM	4:12 AM	8:58 AM	6	6
WED 26	2:54 PM	10:10 PM	4:46 AM	9:46 AM	5	7
THUR 27	3:58 PM	10:55 PM	5:16 AM	10:32 AM	3	8
FRI 28	5:02 PM	11:39 PM	5:42 AM	11:16 AM	○ 5	7
SAT 29	6:06 PM		6:06 AM	12:01 PM	7	6
SUN 30	7:11 PM	12:23 AM	6:30 AM	12:45 PM	7	6
MON 31	8:17 PM	1:07 AM	6:54 AM	1:30 PM	5	5

Apogee moon phase on Saturday 19th
Perigee moon phase on Monday 7th
● New moon on Friday 11th
First quarter moon on Saturday 19th
○ Full moon on Sunday 27th
Last quarter moon phase on Friday 4th

Adelaide, SA: Rise: 06:10am Set: 06:00pm

(Note: These sun rise/set times are averages for the month)

DAY	MINOR BITE	MAJOR BITE	MINOR BITE	MAJOR BITE	SALT WATER RATING	FRESH WATER RATING
TUE 1	9:27 PM	1:53 AM	7:20 AM	2:18 PM	4	4
WED 2	10:39 PM	2:43 AM	7:51 AM	3:09 PM	3	6
THUR 3	11:52 PM	3:37 AM	8:28 AM	4:06 PM	4	4
FRI 4		4:35 AM	9:13 AM	5:05 PM	5	5
SAT 5	1:02 AM	5:36 AM	10:09 AM	6:07 PM	6	6
SUN 6	2:06 AM	6:39 AM	11:15 AM	7:10 PM	7	7
MON 7	3:00 AM	7:41 AM	12:28 PM	8:10 PM	7	8
TUE 8	3:44 AM	8:40 AM	1:43 PM	9:07 PM	5	8
WED 9	4:20 AM	9:34 AM	2:57 PM	9:59 PM	6	7
THUR 10	4:50 AM	10:25 AM	4:08 PM	10:48 PM	8	8
FRI 11	5:17 AM	11:12 AM	5:17 PM	11:34 PM	● 8	8

POPULAR LOCATION ADJUSTMENTS (See full list on page 7)

DAY	MINOR BITE	MAJOR BITE	MINOR BITE	MAJOR BITE	SALT WATER RATING	FRESH WATER RATING
AT 12	5:42 AM	11:58 AM	6:24 PM		8	6
UN 13	6:07 AM	12:43 PM	7:29 PM	12:20 AM	7	6
ON 14	6:32 AM	1:28 PM	8:34 PM	1:05 AM	6	7
UE 15	7:00 AM	2:15 PM	9:39 PM	1:51 AM	5	5
ED 16	7:32 AM	3:03 PM	10:42 PM	2:38 AM	5	5
HUR 17	8:09 AM	3:53 PM	11:42 PM	3:28 AM	4	6
RI 18	8:52 AM	4:44 PM		4:18 AM	3	5
AT 19	9:42 AM	5:35 PM	12:37 AM	5:09 AM	4	6
UN 20	10:38 AM	6:26 PM	1:26 AM	6:00 AM	5	6
ON 21	11:37 AM	7:15 PM	2:09 AM	6:50 AM	4	5
UE 22	12:40 PM	8:03 PM	2:45 AM	7:39 AM	3	5
ED 23	1:43 PM	8:48 PM	3:16 AM	8:25 AM	6	6
HUR 24	2:47 PM	9:33 PM	3:43 AM	9:10 AM	5	7
RI 25	3:51 PM	10:17 PM	4:08 AM	9:54 AM	3	8
AT 26	4:57 PM	11:02 PM	4:32 AM	10:39 AM	3	8
UN 27	6:04 PM	11:48 PM	4:57 AM	11:24 AM	○ 5	7
ON 28	7:14 PM		5:23 AM	12:13 PM	7	6
UE 29	8:27 PM	12:38 AM	5:53 AM	1:04 PM	7	6
ED 30	9:41 PM	1:31 AM	6:28 AM	2:00 PM	5	5

Apogee moon phase on Saturday 17th
Perigee moon phase on Friday 2nd and Thursday 29th
● New moon on Sunday 11th
First quarter moon on Monday 19th
○ Full moon on Monday 26th
Last quarter moon phase on Saturday 3rd

Adelaide, SA: Rise: 06:30am Set: 07:20pm

Note: Daylight Savings start (clocks turn forward 1 hour) on Sunday, October 5th at 2:00 AM. Subtract 1 hour to rise/set time for days before October 1st. These sun rise/set times are averages for the mont

DAY	MINOR BITE	MAJOR BITE	MINOR BITE	MAJOR BITE	SALT WATER RATING	FRESH WATE RATING
THUR 1	10:54 PM	2:29 AM	7:11 AM	2:59 PM	4	4
FRI 2		3:30 AM	8:04 AM	4:01 PM	3	6
SAT 3		4:33 AM	9:07 AM	5:03 PM	5	5
SUN 4	12:57 AM	5:35 AM	10:17 AM	6:04 PM	6	6
MON 5	1:43 AM	6:34 AM	11:31 AM	7:00 PM	7	7
TUE 6	2:20 AM	7:28 AM	12:44 PM	7:52 PM	7	7
WED 7	2:52 AM	8:18 AM	1:54 PM	8:41 PM	7	8
THUR 8	3:19 AM	9:06 AM	3:02 PM	9:28 PM	5	8
FRI 9	3:44 AM	9:51 AM	4:08 PM	10:13 PM	6	7
SAT 10	4:08 AM	10:36 AM	5:13 PM	10:57 PM	8	8
SUN 11	4:33 AM	11:20 AM	6:18 PM	11:42 PM	● 8	8

OCTOBER 2026

POPULAR LOCATION ADJUSTMENTS (See full list on page 7)

DAY	MINOR BITE	MAJOR BITE	MINOR BITE	MAJOR BITE	SALT WATER RATING	FRESH WATER RATING
ON 12	5:00 AM	12:06 PM	7:23 PM		8	6
UE 13	5:30 AM	12:54 PM	8:27 PM	12:30 AM	7	6
ED 14	6:05 AM	1:44 PM	9:29 PM	1:19 AM	6	7
HUR 15	6:46 AM	2:35 PM	10:27 PM	2:09 AM	5	5
RI 16	7:34 AM	3:26 PM	11:19 PM	3:00 AM	4	6
AT 17	8:27 AM	4:17 PM		3:51 AM	3	5
UN 18	9:25 AM	5:07 PM	12:03 AM	4:42 AM	3	5
ON 19	10:26 AM	5:55 PM	12:42 AM	5:30 AM	4	6
UE 20	11:28 AM	6:40 PM	1:14 AM	6:17 AM	5	6
ED 21	12:30 PM	7:25 PM	1:43 AM	7:02 AM	4	5
HUR 22	1:34 PM	8:08 PM	2:08 AM	7:46 AM	3	5
RI 23	2:38 PM	8:52 PM	2:32 AM	8:30 AM	6	6
AT 24	3:44 PM	9:38 PM	2:57 AM	9:15 AM	5	7
UN 25	4:54 PM	10:27 PM	3:22 AM	10:02 AM	3	8
ON 26	6:07 PM	11:20 PM	3:51 AM	10:53 AM	5	7
UE 27	7:23 PM		4:25 AM	11:48 AM	7	6
ED 28	8:39 PM	12:17 AM	5:06 AM	12:48 PM	7	6
HUR 29	9:50 PM	1:20 AM	5:57 AM	1:52 PM	5	5
RI 30	10:51 PM	2:24 AM	6:58 AM	2:56 PM	4	4
AT 31	11:41 PM	3:28 AM	8:08 AM	3:58 PM	3	6

Apogee moon phase on Saturday 14th

Perigee moon phase on Thursday 26th

● **New moon on Monday 9th**

First quarter moon on Tuesday 17th

○ **Full moon on Wednesday 25th**

Last quarter moon phase on Monday 2nd

Adelaide, SA: Rise: 06:00am Set: 07:50pm

(Note: These sun rise/set times are averages for the month)

DAY	MINOR BITE	MAJOR BITE	MINOR BITE	MAJOR BITE	SALT WATER RATING	FRESH WATE RATING
SUN 1		4:29 AM	9:22 AM	4:56 PM	4	4
MON 2	12:22 AM	5:25 AM	10:35 AM	5:50 PM	5	5
TUE 3	12:54 AM	6:16 AM	11:46 AM	6:39 PM	6	6
WED 4	1:23 AM	7:03 AM	12:54 PM	7:25 PM	7	7
THUR 5	1:48 AM	7:48 AM	1:59 PM	8:10 PM	7	8
FRI 6	2:12 AM	8:32 AM	3:03 PM	8:53 PM	5	8
SAT 7	2:36 AM	9:16 AM	4:07 PM	9:38 PM	6	7
SUN 8	3:02 AM	10:01 AM	5:11 PM	10:24 PM	8	8
MON 9	3:31 AM	10:48 AM	6:15 PM	11:12 PM	● 8	8
TUE 10	4:04 AM	11:37 AM	7:17 PM		8	6
WED 11	4:43 AM	12:27 PM	8:17 PM	12:02 AM	7	6

NOVEMBER 2026

POPULAR LOCATION ADJUSTMENTS (See full list on page 7)

DAY	MINOR BITE	MAJOR BITE	MINOR BITE	MAJOR BITE	SALT WATER RATING	FRESH WATER RATING
HUR 12	5:28 AM	1:19 PM	9:11 PM	12:53 AM	7	6
RI 13	6:19 AM	2:10 PM	9:58 PM	1:44 AM	6	7
AT 14	7:15 AM	3:00 PM	10:38 PM	2:35 AM	5	5
UN 15	8:15 AM	3:48 PM	11:13 PM	3:23 AM	4	6
MON 16	9:16 AM	4:34 PM	11:42 PM	4:11 AM	3	5
UE 17	10:17 AM	5:18 PM		4:56 AM	4	6
WED 18	11:18 AM	6:00 PM	12:08 AM	5:39 AM	5	6
HUR 19	12:20 PM	6:43 PM	12:32 AM	6:21 AM	4	5
RI 20	1:24 PM	7:27 PM	12:56 AM	7:04 AM	3	5
SAT 21	2:30 PM	8:13 PM	1:20 AM	7:49 AM	6	6
SUN 22	3:41 PM	9:04 PM	1:47 AM	8:38 AM	5	7
MON 23	4:55 PM	9:59 PM	2:18 AM	9:31 AM	5	7
TUE 24	6:13 PM	11:00 PM	2:55 AM	10:29 AM	3	8
WED 25	7:29 PM		3:43 AM	11:33 AM	5	7
HUR 26	8:37 PM	12:06 AM	4:41 AM	12:39 PM	7	6
FRI 27	9:34 PM	1:13 AM	5:51 AM	1:45 PM	5	5
SAT 28	10:19 PM	2:18 AM	7:06 AM	2:47 PM	4	4
SUN 29	10:56 PM	3:17 AM	8:23 AM	3:44 PM	3	6
MON 30	11:26 PM	4:12 AM	9:36 AM	4:36 PM	4	4

Apogee moon phase on Friday 11th
Perigee moon phase on Thursday 24th
● New moon on Wednesday 9th
First quarter moon on Thursday 17th
○ Full moon on Thursday 24th
Last quarter moon phase on Tuesday 1st and Thursday 31st

Adelaide, SA: Rise: 05:50am Set: 08:20pm

(Note: These sun rise/set times are averages for the month)

DAY	MINOR BITE	MAJOR BITE	MINOR BITE	MAJOR BITE	SALT WATER RATING	FRESH WATE RATING
TUE 1	11:52 PM	5:01 AM	10:46 AM	5:23 PM	5	5
WED 2		5:47 AM	11:52 AM	6:08 PM	6	6
THUR 3	12:16 AM	6:31 AM	12:57 PM	6:52 PM	7	7
FRI 4	12:40 AM	7:15 AM	2:00 PM	7:37 PM	7	8
SAT 5	1:05 AM	7:59 AM	3:03 PM	8:22 PM	7	8
SUN 6	1:33 AM	8:45 AM	4:06 PM	9:08 PM	5	8
MON 7	2:04 AM	9:32 AM	5:08 PM	9:56 PM	6	7
TUE 8	2:41 AM	10:22 AM	6:09 PM	10:47 PM	8	8
WED 9	3:24 AM	11:13 AM	7:04 PM	11:38 PM	● 8	8
THUR 10	4:13 AM	12:05 PM	7:54 PM		8	6
FRI 11	5:08 AM	12:55 PM	8:37 PM	12:30 AM	7	6

DECEMBER 2026

POPULAR LOCATION ADJUSTMENTS (See full list on page 7)

DAY	MINOR BITE	MAJOR BITE	MINOR BITE	MAJOR BITE	SALT WATER RATING	FRESH WATER RATING
AT 12	6:07 AM	1:44 PM	9:13 PM	1:19 AM	6	7
UN 13	7:07 AM	2:30 PM	9:43 PM	2:07 AM	6	7
ION 14	8:08 AM	3:14 PM	10:10 PM	2:52 AM	5	5
UE 15	9:08 AM	3:56 PM	10:34 PM	3:35 AM	4	6
VED 16	10:08 AM	4:38 PM	10:57 PM	4:16 AM	3	5
HUR 17	11:09 AM	5:20 PM	11:21 PM	4:59 AM	4	6
RI 18	12:12 PM	6:03 PM	11:45 PM	5:41 AM	5	6
AT 19	1:18 PM	6:50 PM		6:26 AM	4	5
UN 20	2:29 PM	7:41 PM	12:13 AM	7:15 AM	3	5
ION 21	3:43 PM	8:38 PM	12:46 AM	8:09 AM	6	6
UE 22	4:59 PM	9:41 PM	1:27 AM	9:09 AM	5	7
VED 23	6:12 PM	10:48 PM	2:19 AM	10:14 AM	3	8
HUR 24	7:17 PM	11:56 PM	3:24 AM	11:22 AM	5	7
RI 25	8:09 PM		4:39 AM	12:28 PM	7	6
AT 26	8:51 PM	1:00 AM	5:58 AM	1:29 PM	7	6
UN 27	9:25 PM	1:59 AM	7:16 AM	2:26 PM	5	5
ION 28	9:53 PM	2:53 AM	8:31 AM	3:17 PM	4	4
UE 29	10:19 PM	3:42 AM	9:41 AM	4:04 PM	3	6
VED 30	10:44 PM	4:28 AM	10:48 AM	4:50 PM	4	4
HUR 31	11:09 PM	5:13 AM	11:52 AM	5:34 PM	5	5

Port Lincoln

POPULAR TIDE ADJUSTMENTS

Arno Bay	+ 1hr 4min
Cape Catastrophe	- 30min
Ceduna	- 2hr 30min
Coffin Bay	+ 1hr 30min
Elliston/Cape Finnis	- 45min
Louth Bay	+ 8min
Marion Bay	+ 17min
Port Augusta	+ 6hr
Port Neill	+ 48min
Smoky Bay	- 35min
Streaky Bay	- 25min
Tumby Bay	+ 25min
Whyalla	+ 5hr
Port Victoria	+ 1hr 15min
Franklin Harbour	+ 2hr 40min
Cape Jervis	+ 2hr 5min
Wedge Island	+ 10min
Vivonne Bay	- 1hr 30min
Penneshaw	+ 1hr 20min
American River	+ 2hr 15min
Althorpe Island	+ 14min
Stenhouse Bay	+ 13min
Port Pirie	+ 5hr 30min

Day	Date		Tide 1		
Mon	1		5:25 AM	(1.32)	H
Tue	2		5:49 AM	(1.21)	H
Wed	3		11:35 AM	(1.25)	H
Thu	4		2:59 AM	(0.89)	H
Fri	5		2:19 AM	(0.91)	H
Sat	6		2:16 AM	(0.98)	H
Sun	7		2:27 AM	(1.08)	H
Mon	8	○	2:41 AM	(1.19)	H
Tue	9		2:57 AM	(1.31)	H
Wed	10		3:13 AM	(1.43)	H
Thu	11		3:29 AM	(1.52)	H
Fri	12		3:47 AM	(1.58)	H
Sat	13		4:07 AM	(1.59)	H
Sun	14		4:29 AM	(1.54)	H
Mon	15		4:54 AM	(1.42)	H
Tue	16		5:16 AM	(1.25)	H
Wed	17		5:27 AM	(1.05)	H
Thu	18		2:41 AM	(0.89)	H
Fri	19		2:01 AM	(0.93)	H
Sat	20		1:53 AM	(1.03)	H
Sun	21		2:00 AM	(1.16)	H
Mon	22	●	2:12 AM	(1.30)	H
Tue	23		2:26 AM	(1.43)	H
Wed	24		2:44 AM	(1.53)	H
Thu	25		3:04 AM	(1.60)	H
Fri	26		3:24 AM	(1.63)	H
Sat	27		3:45 AM	(1.61)	H
Sun	28		4:05 AM	(1.55)	H
Mon	29		4:25 AM	(1.46)	H
Tue	30		4:45 AM	(1.34)	H

Tide 2		Tide 3		Tide 4	
12:08 PM	(0.93) L	2:01 PM	(0.97) **H**	9:40 PM	(0.46) L
8:30 AM	(1.13) L	9:16 AM	(1.14) **H**	8:55 PM	(0.47) L
8:11 PM	(0.43) L				
4:14 AM	(0.88) L	12:32 PM	(1.39) **H**	8:02 PM	(0.36) L
6:47 AM	(0.74) L	1:08 PM	(1.52) **H**	8:10 PM	(0.29) L
7:26 AM	(0.57) L	1:41 PM	(1.62) **H**	8:26 PM	(0.24) L
7:59 AM	(0.42) L	2:11 PM	(1.66) **H**	8:44 PM	(0.22) L
8:31 AM	(0.30) L	2:39 PM	(1.63) **H**	9:01 PM	(0.23) L
9:00 AM	(0.24) L	3:03 PM	(1.53) **H**	9:15 PM	(0.25) L
9:29 AM	(0.25) L	3:22 PM	(1.37) **H**	9:23 PM	(0.28) L
9:57 AM	(0.32) L	3:36 PM	(1.19) **H**	9:22 PM	(0.30) L
10:23 AM	(0.45) L	3:41 PM	(1.02) **H**	9:14 PM	(0.28) L
10:47 AM	(0.60) L	3:27 PM	(0.90) **H**	9:10 PM	(0.25) L
11:10 AM	(0.77) L	1:47 PM	(0.91) **H**	9:09 PM	(0.24) L
11:31 AM	(0.94) L	1:28 PM	(0.99) **H**	8:59 PM	(0.27) L
8:38 PM	(0.32) L				
7:18 AM	(1.01) L	12:32 PM	(1.23) **H**	8:05 PM	(0.36) L
7:00 AM	(0.83) L	12:51 PM	(1.33) **H**	7:52 PM	(0.36) L
7:11 AM	(0.65) L	1:13 PM	(1.39) **H**	7:53 PM	(0.36) L
7:30 AM	(0.50) L	1:35 PM	(1.42) **H**	8:00 PM	(0.33) L
7:53 AM	(0.37) L	1:55 PM	(1.43) **H**	8:12 PM	(0.30) L
8:18 AM	(0.28) L	2:16 PM	(1.41) **H**	8:25 PM	(0.27) L
8:42 AM	(0.24) L	2:36 PM	(1.37) **H**	8:39 PM	(0.25) L
9:07 AM	(0.23) L	2:56 PM	(1.30) **H**	8:51 PM	(0.24) L
9:31 AM	(0.26) L	3:15 PM	(1.22) **H**	9:01 PM	(0.24) L
9:55 AM	(0.33) L	3:34 PM	(1.12) **H**	9:10 PM	(0.27) L
10:19 AM	(0.42) L	3:48 PM	(1.01) **H**	9:14 PM	(0.30) L
10:44 AM	(0.54) L	3:50 PM	(0.91) **H**	9:14 PM	(0.35) L
11:10 AM	(0.68) L	2:12 PM	(0.85) **H**	9:10 PM	(0.40) L
11:43 AM	(0.82) L	1:41 PM	(0.86) **H**	8:51 PM	(0.44) L

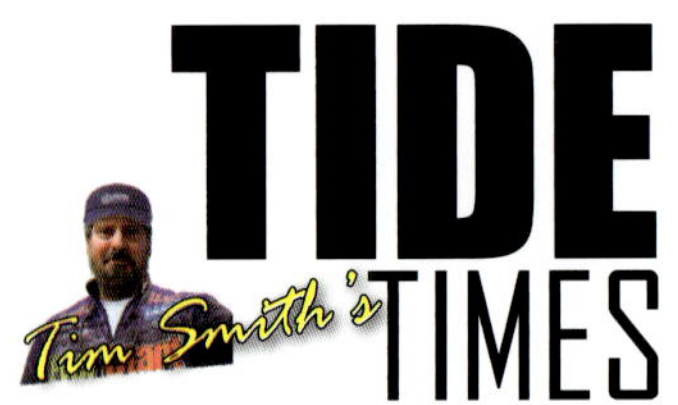

POPULAR TIDE ADJUSTMENTS

Arno Bay	+ 1hr 4min
Cape Catastrophe	- 30min
Ceduna	- 2hr 30min
Coffin Bay	+ 1hr 30min
Elliston/Cape Finnis	- 45min
Louth Bay	+ 8min
Marion Bay	+ 17min
Port Augusta	+ 6hr
Port Neill	+ 48min
Smoky Bay	- 35min
Streaky Bay	- 25min
Tumby Bay	+ 25min
Whyalla	+ 5hr
Port Victoria	+ 1hr 15min
Franklin Harbour	+ 2hr 40min
Cape Jervis	+ 2hr 5min
Wedge Island	+ 10min
Vivonne Bay	- 1hr 30min
Penneshaw	+ 1hr 20min
American River	+ 2hr 15min
Althorpe Island	+ 14min
Stenhouse Bay	+ 13min
Port Pirie	+ 5hr 30min

*** Additional Tides**
Additional tide occur in this month on Saturday the 30th at: **10:32 AM** (1.0) **H** and at: **7:17 PM** (0.3) L

Port Lincoln

Day	Date		Tide 1
Wed	1		5:05 AM (1.20) **H**
Thu	2		5:25 AM (1.04) **H**
Fri	3		2:06 AM (0.93) **H**
Sat	4		1:36 AM (0.99) **H**
Sun	5		1:35 AM (1.11) **H**
Mon	6		2:46 AM (1.25) **H**
Tue	7	○	3:01 AM (1.41) **H**
Wed	8		3:18 AM (1.55) **H**
Thu	9		3:36 AM (1.66) **H**
Fri	10		3:54 AM (1.73) **H**
Sat	11		4:14 AM (1.74) **H**
Sun	12		4:37 AM (1.67) **H**
Mon	13		5:01 AM (1.55) **H**
Tue	14		5:24 AM (1.37) **H**
Wed	15		5:41 AM (1.17) **H**
Thu	16		5:32 AM (0.98) **H**
Fri	17		2:35 AM (0.94) **H**
Sat	18		2:05 AM (1.05) **H**
Sun	19		2:06 AM (1.20) **H**
Mon	20		2:16 AM (1.35) **H**
Tue	21	●	2:31 AM (1.49) **H**
Wed	22		2:50 AM (1.60) **H**
Thu	23		3:12 AM (1.68) **H**
Fri	24		3:33 AM (1.72) **H**
Sat	25		3:55 AM (1.72) **H**
Sun	26		4:17 AM (1.67) **H**
Mon	27		4:39 AM (1.59) **H**
Tue	28		5:01 AM (1.49) **H**
Wed	29		5:24 AM (1.36) **H**
Thu	30		5:47 AM (1.21) **H**
Fri	31		6:09 AM (1.03) **H**

OCTOBER 2025

Tide 2		Tide 3		Tide 4	
7:46 PM	(0.44) L				
7:16 AM	(1.01) L	11:10 AM	(1.13) H	7:18 PM	(0.40) L
6:36 AM	(0.85) L	12:09 PM	(1.27) H	7:16 PM	(0.33) L
6:49 AM	(0.66) L	12:46 PM	(1.38) H	7:27 PM	(0.28) L
8:17 AM	(0.47) L	2:19 PM	(1.43) H	8:44 PM	(0.25) L
8:48 AM	(0.30) L	2:51 PM	(1.42) H	9:01 PM	(0.25) L
9:20 AM	(0.19) L	3:20 PM	(1.35) H	9:15 PM	(0.27) L
9:50 AM	(0.15) L	3:44 PM	(1.21) H	9:23 PM	(0.29) L
10:20 AM	(0.19) L	4:01 PM	(1.04) H	9:23 PM	(0.29) L
10:47 AM	(0.29) L	4:08 PM	(0.88) H	9:16 PM	(0.26) L
11:13 AM	(0.43) L	4:06 PM	(0.77) H	9:16 PM	(0.22) L
11:35 AM	(0.60) L	2:20 PM	(0.76) H	9:23 PM	(0.21) L
11:54 AM	(0.75) L	2:10 PM	(0.84) H	9:24 PM	(0.24) L
9:13 PM	(0.32) L				
12:36 PM	(0.99) L	1:31 PM	(0.99) L	8:42 PM	(0.41) L
8:09 AM	(0.91) L	12:54 PM	(1.07) H	8:01 PM	(0.45) L
7:48 AM	(0.75) L	1:18 PM	(1.12) H	7:53 PM	(0.45) L
7:57 AM	(0.59) L	1:41 PM	(1.15) H	7:56 PM	(0.41) L
8:15 AM	(0.45) L	2:05 PM	(1.17) H	8:07 PM	(0.37) L
8:37 AM	(0.34) L	2:28 PM	(1.18) H	8:21 PM	(0.33) L
9:01 AM	(0.25) L	2:51 PM	(1.17) H	8:38 PM	(0.30) L
9:27 AM	(0.20) L	3:16 PM	(1.14) H	8:52 PM	(0.28) L
9:52 AM	(0.19) L	3:38 PM	(1.08) H	9:06 PM	(0.28) L
10:17 AM	(0.22) L	3:59 PM	(1.02) H	9:19 PM	(0.28) L
10:42 AM	(0.29) L	4:18 PM	(0.95) H	9:29 PM	(0.30) L
11:07 AM	(0.37) L	4:33 PM	(0.87) H	9:37 PM	(0.33) L
11:33 AM	(0.48) L	4:39 PM	(0.79) H	9:43 PM	(0.38) L
12:04 PM	(0.59) L	3:09 PM	(0.73) H	9:43 PM	(0.44) L
9:13 PM	(0.50) L				
7:39 PM	(0.50) L				
8:11 AM	(1.01) L	10:28 AM	(1.03) H	7:11 PM	(0.46) L

POPULAR TIDE ADJUSTMENTS

Arno Bay	+ 1hr 4min
Cape Catastrophe	- 30min
Ceduna	- 2hr 30min
Coffin Bay	+ 1hr 30min
Elliston/Cape Finnis	- 45min
Louth Bay	+ 8min
Marion Bay	+ 17min
Port Augusta	+ 6hr
Port Neill	+ 48min
Smoky Bay	- 35min
Streaky Bay	- 25min
Tumby Bay	+ 25min
Whyalla	+ 5hr
Port Victoria	+ 1hr 15min
Franklin Harbour	+ 2hr 40min
Cape Jervis	+ 2hr 5min
Wedge Island	+ 10min
Vivonne Bay	- 1hr 30min
Penneshaw	+ 1hr 20min
American River	+ 2hr 15min
Althorpe Island	+ 14min
Stenhouse Bay	+ 13min
Port Pirie	+ 5hr 30min

Port Lincoln

Day	Date		Tide 1
Sat	1		2:10 AM (0.96) **H**
Sun	2		1:43 AM (1.08) **H**
Mon	3		1:47 AM (1.25) **H**
Tue	4		2:02 AM (1.43) **H**
Wed	5		2:21 AM (1.60) **H**
Thu	6	○	2:43 AM (1.73) **H**
Fri	7		3:05 AM (1.81) **H**
Sat	8		3:29 AM (1.83) **H**
Sun	9		3:53 AM (1.77) **H**
Mon	10		4:19 AM (1.66) **H**
Tue	11		4:46 AM (1.50) **H**
Wed	12		5:11 AM (1.32) **H**
Thu	13		5:29 AM (1.14) **H**
Fri	14		5:07 AM (0.97) **H**
Sat	15		1:28 AM (0.99) **H**
Sun	16		1:11 AM (1.14) **H**
Mon	17		1:19 AM (1.31) **H**
Tue	18		1:35 AM (1.46) **H**
Wed	19		1:56 AM (1.58) **H**
Thu	20	●	2:20 AM (1.67) **H**
Fri	21		2:46 AM (1.73) **H**
Sat	22		3:11 AM (1.75) **H**
Sun	23		3:37 AM (1.73) **H**
Mon	24		4:02 AM (1.69) **H**
Tue	25		4:28 AM (1.61) **H**
Wed	26		4:55 AM (1.51) **H**
Thu	27		5:23 AM (1.38) **H**
Fri	28		5:53 AM (1.23) **H**
Sat	29		6:33 AM (1.05) **H**
Sun	30		12:46 AM (0.96) **H**

Tide 2		Tide 3		Tide 4	
7:07 AM	(0.83) L	12:22 PM	(1.10) **H**	7:16 PM	(0.41) L
7:31 AM	(0.62) L	1:15 PM	(1.15) **H**	7:32 PM	(0.39) L
8:04 AM	(0.42) L	1:57 PM	(1.16) **H**	7:50 PM	(0.38) L
8:38 AM	(0.27) L	2:34 PM	(1.11) **H**	8:05 PM	(0.39) L
9:11 AM	(0.17) L	3:07 PM	(1.00) **H**	8:14 PM	(0.38) L
9:44 AM	(0.15) L	3:33 PM	(0.87) **H**	8:17 PM	(0.36) L
10:16 AM	(0.20) L	3:49 PM	(0.74) **H**	8:20 PM	(0.32) L
10:46 AM	(0.31) L	3:51 PM	(0.64) **H**	8:28 PM	(0.27) L
11:14 AM	(0.46) L	3:44 PM	(0.61) **H**	8:42 PM	(0.25) L
8:59 PM	(0.28) L				
11:59 AM	(0.69) L	1:54 PM	(0.74) **H**	9:08 PM	(0.36) L
12:25 PM	(0.76) L	1:58 PM	(0.78) **H**	9:00 PM	(0.48) L
7:33 PM	(0.60) L				
6:30 PM	(0.60) L				
7:42 AM	(0.77) L	12:21 PM	(0.87) **H**	6:27 PM	(0.56) L
7:46 AM	(0.62) L	1:03 PM	(0.89) **H**	6:35 PM	(0.52) L
8:03 AM	(0.49) L	1:36 PM	(0.91) **H**	6:55 PM	(0.47) L
8:25 AM	(0.38) L	2:07 PM	(0.92) **H**	7:19 PM	(0.43) L
8:51 AM	(0.29) L	2:37 PM	(0.93) **H**	7:43 PM	(0.40) L
9:17 AM	(0.24) L	3:05 PM	(0.92) **H**	8:07 PM	(0.38) L
9:44 AM	(0.22) L	3:32 PM	(0.90) **H**	8:27 PM	(0.37) L
10:11 AM	(0.24) L	3:56 PM	(0.86) **H**	8:47 PM	(0.36) L
10:38 AM	(0.28) L	4:18 PM	(0.83) **H**	9:05 PM	(0.36) L
11:06 AM	(0.35) L	4:38 PM	(0.78) **H**	9:22 PM	(0.39) L
11:37 AM	(0.41) L	5:00 PM	(0.74) **H**	9:37 PM	(0.44) L
12:12 PM	(0.49) L	5:29 PM	(0.70) **H**	9:50 PM	(0.51) L
12:59 PM	(0.55) L	6:23 PM	(0.67) **H**	9:50 PM	(0.61) L
3:31 PM	(0.59) L				
4:55 PM	(0.58) L				
6:27 AM	(0.84) L	10:12 AM	(0.89) **H**	5:30 PM	(0.56) L

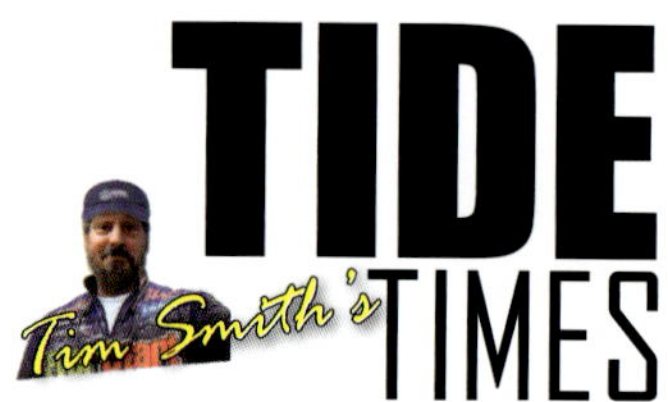

Port Lincoln

Day	Date	Tide 1
Mon	1	12:38 AM (1.14) **H**
Tue	2	12:56 AM (1.34) **H**
Wed	3	1:21 AM (1.52) **H**
Thu	4	1:50 AM (1.68) **H**
Fri	5 ○	2:20 AM (1.78) **H**
Sat	6	2:51 AM (1.82) **H**
Sun	7	3:21 AM (1.80) **H**
Mon	8	3:50 AM (1.72) **H**
Tue	9	4:18 AM (1.60) **H**
Wed	10	4:46 AM (1.46) **H**
Thu	11	5:13 AM (1.31) **H**
Fri	12	5:36 AM (1.15) **H**
Sat	13	5:37 AM (1.00) **H**
Sun	14	2:07 PM (0.56) L
Mon	15	12:05 AM (1.16) **H**
Tue	16	12:31 AM (1.31) **H**
Wed	17	12:59 AM (1.44) **H**
Thu	18	1:30 AM (1.55) **H**
Fri	19	2:01 AM (1.63) **H**
Sat	20 ●	2:33 AM (1.68) **H**
Sun	21	3:05 AM (1.71) **H**
Mon	22	3:36 AM (1.71) **H**
Tue	23	4:06 AM (1.68) **H**
Wed	24	4:35 AM (1.62) **H**
Thu	25	5:03 AM (1.53) **H**
Fri	26	5:31 AM (1.41) **H**
Sat	27	5:57 AM (1.24) **H**
Sun	28	12:42 AM (0.75) L
Mon	29	2:36 AM (0.86) L
Tue	30	11:21 AM (0.54) L
Wed	31	12:06 AM (1.34) **H**

POPULAR TIDE ADJUSTMENTS

Arno Bay	+ 1hr 4min
Cape Catastrophe	- 30min
Ceduna	- 2hr 30min
Coffin Bay	+ 1hr 30min
Elliston/Cape Finnis	- 45min
Louth Bay	+ 8min
Marion Bay	+ 17min
Port Augusta	+ 6hr
Port Neill	+ 48min
Smoky Bay	- 35min
Streaky Bay	- 25min
Tumby Bay	+ 25min
Whyalla	+ 5hr
Port Victoria	+ 1hr 15min
Franklin Harbour	+ 2hr 40min
Cape Jervis	+ 2hr 5min
Wedge Island	+ 10min
Vivonne Bay	- 1hr 30min
Penneshaw	+ 1hr 20min
American River	+ 2hr 15min
Althorpe Island	+ 14min
Stenhouse Bay	+ 13min
Port Pirie	+ 5hr 30min

*** Additional Tides**

Additional tide occur in this month on

Tuesday the 10th at: **4:20 PM** (0.6) L

and at: **11:20 PM** (1.0) **H**

DECEMBER 2025

Tide 2	Tide 3	Tide 4
7:21 AM (0.63) L	12:47 PM (0.86) **H**	5:57 PM (0.55) L
8:02 AM (0.43) L	1:51 PM (0.83) **H**	6:19 PM (0.55) L
8:41 AM (0.28) L	2:39 PM (0.78) **H**	6:40 PM (0.52) L
9:20 AM (0.20) L	3:20 PM (0.71) **H**	7:02 PM (0.49) L
9:57 AM (0.18) L	3:53 PM (0.64) **H**	7:24 PM (0.43) L
10:33 AM (0.23) L	4:17 PM (0.58) **H**	7:47 PM (0.38) L
11:03 AM (0.32) L	4:24 PM (0.55) **H**	8:13 PM (0.34) L
11:29 AM (0.42) L	4:19 PM (0.58) **H**	8:44 PM (0.35) L
11:47 AM (0.50) L	4:35 PM (0.65) **H**	9:17 PM (0.40) L
12:02 PM (0.54) L	5:12 PM (0.72) **H**	9:50 PM (0.50) L
12:19 PM (0.55) L	6:07 PM (0.78) **H**	10:19 PM (0.64) L
12:43 PM (0.55) L	7:33 PM (0.85) **H**	10:21 PM (0.81) L
1:17 PM (0.55) L	11:42 PM (0.99) **H**	
3:48 PM (0.58) L		
8:25 AM (0.55) L	1:37 PM (0.67) **H**	5:14 PM (0.58) L
8:36 AM (0.44) L	2:19 PM (0.71) **H**	6:09 PM (0.56) L
8:57 AM (0.34) L	2:51 PM (0.75) **H**	6:54 PM (0.53) L
9:23 AM (0.28) L	3:20 PM (0.78) **H**	7:33 PM (0.49) L
9:50 AM (0.25) L	3:46 PM (0.79) **H**	8:09 PM (0.45) L
10:17 AM (0.24) L	4:11 PM (0.80) **H**	8:41 PM (0.41) L
10:45 AM (0.25) L	4:35 PM (0.81) **H**	9:11 PM (0.40) L
11:13 AM (0.27) L	5:00 PM (0.82) **H**	9:42 PM (0.41) L
11:40 AM (0.30) L	5:27 PM (0.83) **H**	10:13 PM (0.46) L
12:06 PM (0.33) L	5:58 PM (0.85) **H**	10:48 PM (0.53) L
12:32 PM (0.38) L	6:34 PM (0.88) **H**	11:34 PM (0.63) L
12:57 PM (0.43) L	7:21 PM (0.93) **H**	
6:21 AM (1.05) **H**	1:20 PM (0.49) L	9:08 PM (1.01) **H**
3:57 AM (0.86) L	1:32 PM (0.54) L	11:07 PM (1.16) **H**
9:33 AM (0.41) L		

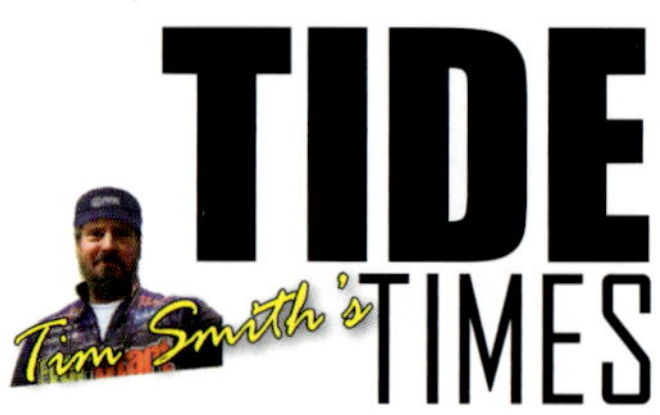

POPULAR TIDE ADJUSTMENTS

Arno Bay	+ 1hr 4min
Cape Catastrophe	- 30min
Ceduna	- 2hr 30min
Coffin Bay	+ 1hr 30min
Elliston/Cape Finnis	- 45min
Louth Bay	+ 8min
Marion Bay	+ 17min
Port Augusta	+ 6hr
Port Neill	+ 48min
Smoky Bay	- 35min
Streaky Bay	- 25min
Tumby Bay	+ 25min
Whyalla	+ 5hr
Port Victoria	+ 1hr 15min
Franklin Harbour	+ 2hr 40min
Cape Jervis	+ 2hr 5min
Wedge Island	+ 10min
Vivonne Bay	- 1hr 30min
Penneshaw	+ 1hr 20min
American River	+ 2hr 15min
Althorpe Island	+ 14min
Stenhouse Bay	+ 13min
Port Pirie	+ 5hr 30min

Port Lincoln

Day	Date		Tide 1		
Thu	1		12:56 AM	(1.50)	H
Fri	2		1:42 AM	(1.63)	H
Sat	3	○	2:26 AM	(1.71)	H
Sun	4		3:05 AM	(1.74)	H
Mon	5		3:39 AM	(1.71)	H
Tue	6		4:05 AM	(1.65)	H
Wed	7		4:28 AM	(1.55)	H
Thu	8		4:50 AM	(1.45)	H
Fri	9		5:12 AM	(1.33)	H
Sat	10		5:31 AM	(1.19)	H
Sun	11		12:29 AM	(0.72)	L
Mon	12		1:23 AM	(0.85)	L
Tue	13		11:58 AM	(0.43)	L
Wed	14		11:11 AM	(0.45)	L
Thu	15		12:34 AM	(1.33)	H
Fri	16		1:20 AM	(1.43)	H
Sat	17		2:01 AM	(1.53)	H
Sun	18		2:39 AM	(1.61)	H
Mon	19	●	3:14 AM	(1.67)	H
Tue	20		3:45 AM	(1.70)	H
Wed	21		4:13 AM	(1.69)	H
Thu	22		4:39 AM	(1.63)	H
Fri	23		5:03 AM	(1.52)	H
Sat	24		5:24 AM	(1.37)	H
Sun	25		5:40 AM	(1.20)	H
Mon	26		12:36 AM	(0.65)	L
Tue	27		1:27 AM	(0.80)	L
Wed	28		11:12 AM	(0.30)	L
Thu	29		10:32 AM	(0.24)	L
Fri	30		1:04 AM	(1.40)	H
Sat	31		2:08 AM	(1.53)	H

Tide 2	Tide 3	Tide 4
9:35 AM (0.26) L	4:03 PM (0.63) H	5:16 PM (0.62) L
10:01 AM (0.18) L	4:11 PM (0.62) H	6:22 PM (0.57) L
10:29 AM (0.16) L	4:25 PM (0.62) H	7:17 PM (0.51) L
10:51 AM (0.20) L	4:40 PM (0.63) H	8:11 PM (0.45) L
11:06 AM (0.26) L	4:52 PM (0.68) H	9:01 PM (0.40) L
11:19 AM (0.32) L	4:59 PM (0.76) H	9:45 PM (0.39) L
11:30 AM (0.35) L	5:09 PM (0.87) H	10:25 PM (0.42) L
11:39 AM (0.35) L	5:31 PM (0.98) H	11:04 PM (0.50) L
11:50 AM (0.33) L	6:03 PM (1.06) H	11:45 PM (0.60) L
12:04 PM (0.32) L	6:41 PM (1.11) H	
5:43 AM (1.05) H	12:20 PM (0.33) L	7:27 PM (1.12) H
4:17 AM (0.93) H	12:27 PM (0.38) L	9:17 PM (1.13) H
11:35 PM (1.22) H		
9:58 AM (0.41) L		
9:37 AM (0.34) L	3:42 PM (0.71) H	6:25 PM (0.64) L
9:43 AM (0.27) L	3:46 PM (0.76) H	7:30 PM (0.57) L
10:00 AM (0.22) L	4:00 PM (0.81) H	8:28 PM (0.49) L
10:20 AM (0.18) L	4:19 PM (0.86) H	9:12 PM (0.41) L
10:42 AM (0.16) L	4:38 PM (0.92) H	9:48 PM (0.36) L
11:03 AM (0.16) L	4:58 PM (0.98) H	10:21 PM (0.35) L
11:23 AM (0.17) L	5:18 PM (1.04) H	10:52 PM (0.37) L
11:40 AM (0.20) L	5:39 PM (1.10) H	11:24 PM (0.43) L
11:53 AM (0.24) L	6:01 PM (1.16) H	11:58 PM (0.53) L
12:00 PM (0.29) L	6:27 PM (1.21) H	
5:48 AM (1.00) H	11:59 AM (0.32) L	6:58 PM (1.23) H
3:52 AM (0.87) H	11:44 AM (0.33) L	7:42 PM (1.21) H
11:31 PM (1.27) H		
10:12 AM (0.18) L		
10:11 AM (0.14) L	4:22 PM (0.70) H	6:50 PM (0.65) L

POPULAR TIDE ADJUSTMENTS

Arno Bay	+ 1hr 4min
Cape Catastrophe	- 30min
Ceduna	- 2hr 30min
Coffin Bay	+ 1hr 30min
Elliston/Cape Finnis	- 45min
Louth Bay	+ 8min
Marion Bay	+ 17min
Port Augusta	+ 6hr
Port Neill	+ 48min
Smoky Bay	- 35min
Streaky Bay	- 25min
Tumby Bay	+ 25min
Whyalla	+ 5hr
Port Victoria	+ 1hr 15min
Franklin Harbour	+ 2hr 40min
Cape Jervis	+ 2hr 5min
Wedge Island	+ 10min
Vivonne Bay	- 1hr 30min
Penneshaw	+ 1hr 20min
American River	+ 2hr 15min
Althorpe Island	+ 14min
Stenhouse Bay	+ 13min
Port Pirie	+ 5hr 30min

Port Lincoln

Day	Date	Tide 1
Sun	1	2:51 AM (1.62) H
Mon	2 ○	3:24 AM (1.65) H
Tue	3	3:49 AM (1.64) H
Wed	4	4:08 AM (1.58) H
Thu	5	4:24 AM (1.50) H
Fri	6	4:41 AM (1.41) H
Sat	7	5:00 AM (1.30) H
Sun	8	5:16 AM (1.19) H
Mon	9	12:13 AM (0.60) L
Tue	10	12:45 AM (0.74) L
Wed	11	1:26 AM (0.88) L
Thu	12	10:57 AM (0.37) L
Fri	13	12:22 AM (1.20) H
Sat	14	1:30 AM (1.32) H
Sun	15	2:12 AM (1.45) H
Mon	16	2:45 AM (1.56) H
Tue	17 ●	3:15 AM (1.63) H
Wed	18	3:42 AM (1.66) H
Thu	19	4:07 AM (1.63) H
Fri	20	4:30 AM (1.54) H
Sat	21	4:49 AM (1.40) H
Sun	22	5:04 AM (1.23) H
Mon	23	5:13 AM (1.06) H
Tue	24	12:18 AM (0.61) L
Wed	25	12:50 AM (0.79) L
Thu	26	10:33 AM (0.21) L
Fri	27	10:07 AM (0.21) L
Sat	28	1:45 AM (1.33) H

Tide 2		Tide 3		Tide 4	
10:19 AM	(0.15) L	4:15 PM	(0.74) **H**	8:42 PM	(0.52) L
10:28 AM	(0.18) L	4:22 PM	(0.82) **H**	9:22 PM	(0.40) L
10:37 AM	(0.20) L	4:31 PM	(0.92) **H**	9:54 PM	(0.33) L
10:47 AM	(0.22) L	4:41 PM	(1.04) **H**	10:22 PM	(0.31) L
10:58 AM	(0.21) L	4:53 PM	(1.17) **H**	10:48 PM	(0.33) L
11:06 AM	(0.18) L	5:12 PM	(1.27) **H**	11:15 PM	(0.39) L
11:15 AM	(0.17) L	5:36 PM	(1.33) **H**	11:42 PM	(0.48) L
11:27 AM	(0.17) L	6:01 PM	(1.35) **H**		
5:28 AM	(1.05) **H**	11:35 AM	(0.22) L	6:28 PM	(1.31) **H**
4:39 AM	(0.93) **H**	11:33 AM	(0.28) L	6:55 PM	(1.24) **H**
3:22 AM	(0.92) **H**	11:19 AM	(0.33) L	7:26 PM	(1.15) **H**
10:03 AM	(0.36) L				
9:36 AM	(0.31) L	3:56 PM	(0.79) **H**	6:31 PM	(0.73) L
9:34 AM	(0.24) L	3:44 PM	(0.84) **H**	8:21 PM	(0.60) L
9:45 AM	(0.18) L	3:49 PM	(0.92) **H**	8:58 PM	(0.46) L
10:01 AM	(0.13) L	4:03 PM	(1.02) **H**	9:29 PM	(0.34) L
10:19 AM	(0.11) L	4:18 PM	(1.12) **H**	9:59 PM	(0.27) L
10:37 AM	(0.11) L	4:35 PM	(1.22) **H**	10:28 PM	(0.24) L
10:51 AM	(0.13) L	4:52 PM	(1.32) **H**	10:55 PM	(0.27) L
11:01 AM	(0.16) L	5:09 PM	(1.40) **H**	11:23 PM	(0.34) L
11:06 AM	(0.19) L	5:28 PM	(1.45) **H**	11:50 PM	(0.46) L
11:03 AM	(0.20) L	5:48 PM	(1.47) **H**		
5:03 AM	(0.90) **H**	10:59 AM	(0.20) L	6:13 PM	(1.43) **H**
3:15 AM	(0.88) **H**	10:52 AM	(0.20) L	6:39 PM	(1.33) **H**
7:04 PM	(1.17) **H**	8:52 PM	(1.14) L	11:35 PM	(1.19) **H**
7:18 PM	(0.98) **H**	8:01 PM	(0.98) L		
9:42 AM	(0.20) L	4:16 PM	(0.81) **H**	8:12 PM	(0.78) L

Port Lincoln

POPULAR TIDE ADJUSTMENTS

Arno Bay	+ 1hr 4min
Cape Catastrophe	- 30min
Ceduna	- 2hr 30min
Coffin Bay	+ 1hr 30min
Elliston/Cape Finnis	- 45min
Louth Bay	+ 8min
Marion Bay	+ 17min
Port Augusta	+ 6hr
Port Neill	+ 48min
Smoky Bay	- 35min
Streaky Bay	- 25min
Tumby Bay	+ 25min
Whyalla	+ 5hr
Port Victoria	+ 1hr 15min
Franklin Harbour	+ 2hr 40min
Cape Jervis	+ 2hr 5min
Wedge Island	+ 10min
Vivonne Bay	- 1hr 30min
Penneshaw	+ 1hr 20min
American River	+ 2hr 15min
Althorpe Island	+ 14min
Stenhouse Bay	+ 13min
Port Pirie	+ 5hr 30min

Day	Date	Tide 1
Sun	1	2:22 AM (1.45) H
Mon	2	2:49 AM (1.51) H
Tue	3 ○	3:14 AM (1.53) H
Wed	4	3:33 AM (1.51) H
Thu	5	3:50 AM (1.46) H
Fri	6	4:06 AM (1.39) H
Sat	7	4:24 AM (1.31) H
Sun	8	4:42 AM (1.22) H
Mon	9	4:59 AM (1.12) H
Tue	10	5:10 AM (1.00) H
Wed	11	12:21 AM (0.66) L
Thu	12	12:51 AM (0.81) L
Fri	13	10:23 AM (0.39) L
Sat	14	9:21 AM (0.39) L
Sun	15	1:22 AM (1.26) H
Mon	16	1:59 AM (1.38) H
Tue	17	2:29 AM (1.48) H
Wed	18	2:58 AM (1.54) H
Thu	19 ●	3:26 AM (1.53) H
Fri	20	3:50 AM (1.46) H
Sat	21	4:12 AM (1.34) H
Sun	22	4:29 AM (1.18) H
Mon	23	4:38 AM (1.02) H
Tue	24	4:39 AM (0.89) H
Wed	25	12:05 AM (0.66) L
Thu	26	12:30 AM (0.84) L
Fri	27	9:49 AM (0.28) L
Sat	28	12:19 AM (1.15) H
Sun	29	1:32 AM (1.25) H
Mon	30	2:00 AM (1.31) H
Tue	31	2:23 AM (1.34) H

Tide 2		Tide 3		Tide 4	
9:36 AM	(0.21) L	3:45 PM	(0.85) **H**	8:35 PM	(0.60) L
9:40 AM	(0.21) L	3:41 PM	(0.95) **H**	9:00 PM	(0.45) L
9:47 AM	(0.22) L	3:47 PM	(1.07) **H**	9:26 PM	(0.33) L
9:58 AM	(0.20) L	3:59 PM	(1.21) **H**	9:51 PM	(0.26) L
10:09 AM	(0.18) L	4:10 PM	(1.34) **H**	10:16 PM	(0.24) L
10:19 AM	(0.16) L	4:25 PM	(1.46) **H**	10:40 PM	(0.27) L
10:28 AM	(0.14) L	4:44 PM	(1.54) **H**	11:03 PM	(0.33) L
10:38 AM	(0.14) L	5:05 PM	(1.57) **H**	11:28 PM	(0.42) L
10:48 AM	(0.17) L	5:28 PM	(1.54) **H**	11:54 PM	(0.53) L
10:54 AM	(0.22) L	5:49 PM	(1.47) **H**		
4:40 AM	(0.90) **H**	10:52 AM	(0.29) L	6:10 PM	(1.37) **H**
3:14 AM	(0.89) **H**	10:44 AM	(0.34) L	6:30 PM	(1.24) **H**
6:47 PM	(1.10) **H**	8:45 PM	(1.06) L	11:56 PM	(1.12) **H**
6:55 PM	(0.94) **H**	8:03 PM	(0.94) L		
8:59 AM	(0.34) L	3:29 PM	(0.90) **H**	8:02 PM	(0.77) L
9:00 AM	(0.28) L	3:15 PM	(0.98) **H**	8:25 PM	(0.60) L
9:12 AM	(0.22) L	3:19 PM	(1.10) **H**	8:53 PM	(0.44) L
9:28 AM	(0.18) L	3:30 PM	(1.23) **H**	9:22 PM	(0.31) L
9:45 AM	(0.17) L	3:45 PM	(1.37) **H**	9:51 PM	(0.23) L
9:59 AM	(0.18) L	4:01 PM	(1.50) **H**	10:19 PM	(0.21) L
10:09 AM	(0.20) L	4:18 PM	(1.61) **H**	10:47 PM	(0.25) L
10:13 AM	(0.21) L	4:36 PM	(1.67) **H**	11:14 PM	(0.35) L
10:11 AM	(0.21) L	4:56 PM	(1.69) **H**	11:40 PM	(0.50) L
10:08 AM	(0.20) L	5:17 PM	(1.64) **H**		
2:58 AM	(0.83) **H**	10:10 AM	(0.20) L	5:41 PM	(1.53) **H**
2:31 AM	(0.90) **H**	10:07 AM	(0.23) L	6:04 PM	(1.37) **H**
6:20 PM	(1.17) **H**	8:46 PM	(1.10) L		
9:15 AM	(0.34) L	6:11 PM	(0.97) **H**	8:05 PM	(0.94) L
8:47 AM	(0.36) L	3:15 PM	(0.94) **H**	8:08 PM	(0.75) L
8:45 AM	(0.36) L	2:55 PM	(1.04) **H**	8:26 PM	(0.59) L
8:50 AM	(0.35) L	2:57 PM	(1.18) **H**	8:47 PM	(0.45) L

POPULAR TIDE ADJUSTMENTS

Arno Bay	+ 1hr 4min
Cape Catastrophe	- 30min
Ceduna	- 2hr 30min
Coffin Bay	+ 1hr 30min
Elliston/Cape Finnis	- 45min
Louth Bay	+ 8min
Marion Bay	+ 17min
Port Augusta	+ 6hr
Port Neill	+ 48min
Smoky Bay	- 35min
Streaky Bay	- 25min
Tumby Bay	+ 25min
Whyalla	+ 5hr
Port Victoria	+ 1hr 15min
Franklin Harbour	+ 2hr 40min
Cape Jervis	+ 2hr 5min
Wedge Island	+ 10min
Vivonne Bay	- 1hr 30min
Penneshaw	+ 1hr 20min
American River	+ 2hr 15min
Althorpe Island	+ 14min
Stenhouse Bay	+ 13min
Port Pirie	+ 5hr 30min

Port Lincoln

Day	Date	Tide 1
Wed	1	2:45 AM (1.34) **H**
Thu	2 ○	3:06 AM (1.32) **H**
Fri	3	3:26 AM (1.29) **H**
Sat	4	3:45 AM (1.24) **H**
Sun	5	3:05 AM (1.18) **H**
Mon	6	3:25 AM (1.11) **H**
Tue	7	3:42 AM (1.02) **H**
Wed	8	3:53 AM (0.94) **H**
Thu	9	3:38 AM (0.86) **H**
Fri	10	1:55 AM (0.85) **H**
Sat	11	8:36 AM (0.52) L
Sun	12	7:19 AM (0.51) L
Mon	13	7:04 AM (0.46) L
Tue	14	12:20 AM (1.29) **H**
Wed	15	12:59 AM (1.35) **H**
Thu	16	1:33 AM (1.36) **H**
Fri	17 ●	2:04 AM (1.31) **H**
Sat	18	2:32 AM (1.21) **H**
Sun	19	2:54 AM (1.07) **H**
Mon	20	3:08 AM (0.92) **H**
Tue	21	3:11 AM (0.81) **H**
Wed	22	1:32 AM (0.75) **H**
Thu	23	1:02 AM (0.82) **H**
Fri	24	12:48 AM (0.90) **H**
Sat	25	8:05 AM (0.49) L
Sun	26	7:00 AM (0.58) L
Mon	27	6:38 AM (0.59) L
Tue	28	12:15 AM (1.13) **H**
Wed	29	12:44 AM (1.13) **H**
Thu	30	1:11 AM (1.13) **H**

Tide 2		Tide 3		Tide 4	
9:00 AM	(0.32) L	3:06 PM	(1.34) **H**	9:12 PM	(0.35) L
9:12 AM	(0.29) L	3:19 PM	(1.48) **H**	9:36 PM	(0.29) L
9:25 AM	(0.26) L	3:35 PM	(1.61) **H**	10:01 PM	(0.27) L
9:36 AM	(0.24) L	3:54 PM	(1.69) **H**	10:26 PM	(0.29) L
8:47 AM	(0.23) L	3:15 PM	(1.74) **H**	9:49 PM	(0.35) L
9:00 AM	(0.24) L	3:37 PM	(1.73) **H**	10:14 PM	(0.43) L
9:10 AM	(0.27) L	3:59 PM	(1.67) **H**	10:39 PM	(0.53) L
9:16 AM	(0.33) L	4:20 PM	(1.58) **H**	11:07 PM	(0.66) L
9:18 AM	(0.39) L	4:42 PM	(1.47) **H**	11:40 PM	(0.78) L
9:14 AM	(0.46) L	5:02 PM	(1.33) **H**		
5:23 PM	(1.18) **H**	8:00 PM	(1.12) L	9:01 PM	(1.12) L
5:29 PM	(1.01) **H**	6:45 PM	(1.00) L	11:26 PM	(1.20) **H**
1:42 PM	(1.02) **H**	6:41 PM	(0.83) L		
7:10 AM	(0.41) L	1:29 PM	(1.14) **H**	7:06 PM	(0.64) L
7:25 AM	(0.37) L	1:35 PM	(1.30) **H**	7:37 PM	(0.47) L
7:42 AM	(0.35) L	1:49 PM	(1.47) **H**	8:08 PM	(0.34) L
7:58 AM	(0.35) L	2:07 PM	(1.63) **H**	8:40 PM	(0.27) L
8:08 AM	(0.36) L	2:26 PM	(1.76) **H**	9:11 PM	(0.27) L
8:14 AM	(0.35) L	2:46 PM	(1.84) **H**	9:41 PM	(0.34) L
8:14 AM	(0.33) L	3:07 PM	(1.86) **H**	10:09 PM	(0.46) L
8:15 AM	(0.30) L	3:30 PM	(1.81) **H**	10:37 PM	(0.61) L
8:23 AM	(0.29) L	3:56 PM	(1.71) **H**	11:04 PM	(0.76) L
8:31 AM	(0.32) L	4:21 PM	(1.55) **H**	11:35 PM	(0.89) L
8:30 AM	(0.39) L	4:45 PM	(1.36) **H**		
4:59 PM	(1.17) **H**	8:03 PM	(1.10) L	9:02 PM	(1.10) L
4:23 PM	(1.00) **H**	6:45 PM	(0.96) L	11:33 PM	(1.11) **H**
1:10 PM	(1.08) **H**	6:50 PM	(0.80) L		
6:39 AM	(0.57) L	1:00 PM	(1.23) **H**	7:08 PM	(0.66) L
6:45 AM	(0.53) L	1:07 PM	(1.40) **H**	7:30 PM	(0.55) L
6:59 AM	(0.49) L	1:21 PM	(1.55) **H**	7:55 PM	(0.46) L

POPULAR TIDE ADJUSTMENTS

Arno Bay	+ 1hr 4min
Cape Catastrophe	- 30min
Ceduna	- 2hr 30min
Coffin Bay	+ 1hr 30min
Elliston/Cape Finnis	- 45min
Louth Bay	+ 8min
Marion Bay	+ 17min
Port Augusta	+ 6hr
Port Neill	+ 48min
Smoky Bay	- 35min
Streaky Bay	- 25min
Tumby Bay	+ 25min
Whyalla	+ 5hr
Port Victoria	+ 1hr 15min
Franklin Harbour	+ 2hr 40min
Cape Jervis	+ 2hr 5min
Wedge Island	+ 10min
Vivonne Bay	- 1hr 30min
Penneshaw	+ 1hr 20min
American River	+ 2hr 15min
Althorpe Island	+ 14min
Stenhouse Bay	+ 13min
Port Pirie	+ 5hr 30min

Port Lincoln

Day	Date	Tide 1
Fri	1	1:37 AM (1.12) **H**
Sat	2 ○	2:02 AM (1.11) **H**
Sun	3	2:27 AM (1.08) **H**
Mon	4	2:50 AM (1.04) **H**
Tue	5	3:13 AM (1.00) **H**
Wed	6	3:32 AM (0.95) **H**
Thu	7	3:48 AM (0.90) **H**
Fri	8	4:01 AM (0.84) **H**
Sat	9	2:09 AM (0.79) **H**
Sun	10	7:21 AM (0.71) L
Mon	11	5:30 AM (0.67) L
Tue	12	5:37 AM (0.63) L
Wed	13	5:56 AM (0.60) L
Thu	14	12:24 AM (1.14) **H**
Fri	15	1:12 AM (1.11) **H**
Sat	16	1:52 AM (1.04) **H**
Sun	17 ●	2:26 AM (0.94) **H**
Mon	18	2:52 AM (0.83) **H**
Tue	19	3:04 AM (0.73) **H**
Wed	20	3:00 AM (0.69) **H**
Thu	21	12:31 AM (0.72) **H**
Fri	22	12:34 AM (0.80) **H**
Sat	23	8:32 AM (0.62) L
Sun	24	8:17 AM (0.77) L
Mon	25	4:13 AM (0.80) L
Tue	26	3:54 AM (0.76) L
Wed	27	4:15 AM (0.71) L
Thu	28	4:50 AM (0.67) L
Fri	29	12:41 AM (0.93) **H**
Sat	30	1:19 AM (0.95) **H**
Sun	31 ○	1:53 AM (0.96) **H**

Tide 2		Tide 3		Tide 4	
7:15 AM	(0.44) L	1:40 PM	(1.68) **H**	8:20 PM	(0.40) L
7:33 AM	(0.41) L	2:01 PM	(1.78) **H**	8:46 PM	(0.37) L
7:51 AM	(0.39) L	2:25 PM	(1.83) **H**	9:13 PM	(0.38) L
8:08 AM	(0.39) L	2:49 PM	(1.84) **H**	9:39 PM	(0.43) L
8:24 AM	(0.40) L	3:14 PM	(1.81) **H**	10:05 PM	(0.50) L
8:38 AM	(0.42) L	3:38 PM	(1.74) **H**	10:33 PM	(0.58) L
8:50 AM	(0.47) L	4:02 PM	(1.65) **H**	11:06 PM	(0.67) L
9:00 AM	(0.53) L	4:28 PM	(1.54) **H**	11:50 PM	(0.75) L
9:01 AM	(0.62) L	4:55 PM	(1.41) **H**		
5:27 PM	(1.26) **H**				
9:18 PM	(1.15) **H**				
12:33 PM	(1.12) **H**	6:04 PM	(0.90) L	11:19 PM	(1.14) **H**
12:30 PM	(1.29) **H**	6:45 PM	(0.71) L		
6:16 AM	(0.59) L	12:44 PM	(1.48) **H**	7:23 PM	(0.54) L
6:33 AM	(0.58) L	1:05 PM	(1.66) **H**	8:00 PM	(0.42) L
6:46 AM	(0.56) L	1:30 PM	(1.81) **H**	8:36 PM	(0.36) L
6:58 AM	(0.53) L	1:56 PM	(1.91) **H**	9:12 PM	(0.38) L
7:09 AM	(0.49) L	2:23 PM	(1.95) **H**	9:47 PM	(0.45) L
7:22 AM	(0.45) L	2:50 PM	(1.92) **H**	10:22 PM	(0.57) L
7:39 AM	(0.42) L	3:18 PM	(1.83) **H**	10:55 PM	(0.69) L
8:00 AM	(0.44) L	3:46 PM	(1.69) **H**	11:27 PM	(0.79) L
8:20 AM	(0.51) L	4:15 PM	(1.53) **H**		
4:43 PM	(1.36) **H**				
5:02 PM	(1.19) **H**				
1:52 PM	(1.05) **H**	2:15 PM	(1.05) L	4:05 PM	(1.05) L
11:50 AM	(1.20) **H**	6:43 PM	(0.89) L	9:25 PM	(0.94) **H**
11:59 AM	(1.37) **H**	7:00 PM	(0.77) L	11:54 PM	(0.92) **H**
12:16 PM	(1.52) **H**	7:21 PM	(0.66) L		
5:29 AM	(0.63) L	12:40 PM	(1.65) **H**	7:45 PM	(0.57) L
6:06 AM	(0.60) L	1:07 PM	(1.75) **H**	8:13 PM	(0.51) L
6:40 AM	(0.57) L	1:36 PM	(1.82) **H**	8:41 PM	(0.48) L

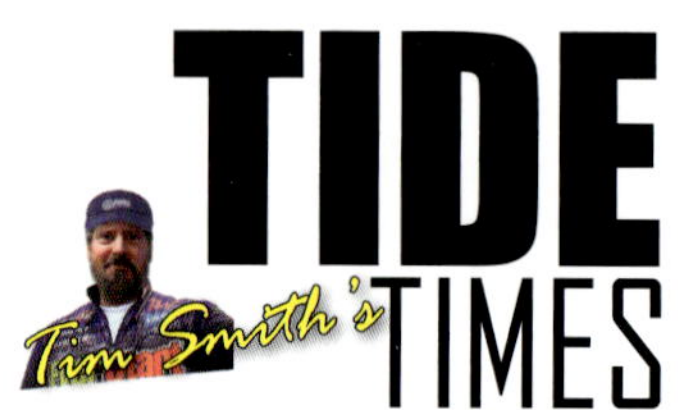

POPULAR TIDE ADJUSTMENTS

Arno Bay	+ 1hr 4min
Cape Catastrophe	- 30min
Ceduna	- 2hr 30min
Coffin Bay	+ 1hr 30min
Elliston/Cape Finnis	- 45min
Louth Bay	+ 8min
Marion Bay	+ 17min
Port Augusta	+ 6hr
Port Neill	+ 48min
Smoky Bay	- 35min
Streaky Bay	- 25min
Tumby Bay	+ 25min
Whyalla	+ 5hr
Port Victoria	+ 1hr 15min
Franklin Harbour	+ 2hr 40min
Cape Jervis	+ 2hr 5min
Wedge Island	+ 10min
Vivonne Bay	- 1hr 30min
Penneshaw	+ 1hr 20min
American River	+ 2hr 15min
Althorpe Island	+ 14min
Stenhouse Bay	+ 13min
Port Pirie	+ 5hr 30min

Port Lincoln

Day	Date	Tide 1
Mon	1	2:23 AM (0.96) **H**
Tue	2	2:51 AM (0.96) **H**
Wed	3	3:16 AM (0.95) **H**
Thu	4	3:41 AM (0.93) **H**
Fri	5	4:08 AM (0.92) **H**
Sat	6	4:41 AM (0.91) **H**
Sun	7	5:25 AM (0.91) **H**
Mon	8	12:31 AM (0.69) L
Tue	9	1:28 AM (0.72) L
Wed	10	2:34 AM (0.73) L
Thu	11	3:29 AM (0.74) L
Fri	12	12:03 AM (0.90) **H**
Sat	13	1:21 AM (0.86) **H**
Sun	14	2:15 AM (0.82) **H**
Mon	15 ●	2:57 AM (0.77) **H**
Tue	16	3:29 AM (0.73) **H**
Wed	17	3:52 AM (0.70) **H**
Thu	18	4:00 AM (0.72) **H**
Fri	19	3:58 AM (0.79) **H**
Sat	20	4:20 AM (0.89) **H**
Sun	21	5:00 AM (0.98) **H**
Mon	22	5:54 AM (1.07) **H**
Tue	23	7:13 AM (1.15) **H**
Wed	24	12:26 AM (0.65) L
Thu	25	1:03 AM (0.68) L
Fri	26	2:13 AM (0.72) L
Sat	27	1:08 AM (0.78) **H**
Sun	28	1:46 AM (0.83) **H**
Mon	29	2:15 AM (0.88) **H**
Tue	30 ○	2:42 AM (0.91) **H**

Tide 2		Tide 3		Tide 4	
7:11 AM	(0.55) L	2:05 PM	(1.85) **H**	9:09 PM	(0.48) L
7:38 AM	(0.53) L	2:34 PM	(1.85) **H**	9:38 PM	(0.50) L
8:03 AM	(0.53) L	3:02 PM	(1.82) **H**	10:07 PM	(0.54) L
8:27 AM	(0.54) L	3:30 PM	(1.77) **H**	10:38 PM	(0.58) L
8:49 AM	(0.58) L	3:59 PM	(1.69) **H**	11:11 PM	(0.62) L
9:12 AM	(0.65) L	4:28 PM	(1.59) **H**	11:47 PM	(0.66) L
9:34 AM	(0.75) L	4:59 PM	(1.47) **H**		
6:38 AM	(0.93) **H**	9:58 AM	(0.87) L	5:35 PM	(1.32) **H**
9:28 AM	(1.02) **H**	12:46 PM	(1.01) L	6:32 PM	(1.14) **H**
10:45 AM	(1.20) **H**	5:37 PM	(0.93) L	8:38 PM	(0.98) **H**
11:18 AM	(1.39) **H**	6:41 PM	(0.75) L		
4:12 AM	(0.74) L	11:54 AM	(1.58) **H**	7:29 PM	(0.58) L
4:49 AM	(0.72) L	12:30 PM	(1.74) **H**	8:13 PM	(0.47) L
5:24 AM	(0.69) L	1:07 PM	(1.86) **H**	8:57 PM	(0.41) L
5:59 AM	(0.64) L	1:45 PM	(1.92) **H**	9:38 PM	(0.42) L
6:32 AM	(0.59) L	2:20 PM	(1.92) **H**	10:15 PM	(0.48) L
7:07 AM	(0.55) L	2:53 PM	(1.87) **H**	10:44 PM	(0.57) L
7:43 AM	(0.54) L	3:22 PM	(1.77) **H**	11:00 PM	(0.65) L
8:21 AM	(0.57) L	3:49 PM	(1.65) **H**	11:12 PM	(0.70) L
9:05 AM	(0.65) L	4:15 PM	(1.51) **H**	11:22 PM	(0.70) L
9:58 AM	(0.77) L	4:40 PM	(1.37) **H**	11:35 PM	(0.68) L
11:06 AM	(0.90) L	4:59 PM	(1.23) **H**	11:57 PM	(0.65) L
12:32 PM	(1.03) L	4:24 PM	(1.10) **H**		
9:45 AM	(1.26) **H**				
10:51 AM	(1.39) **H**				
11:33 AM	(1.52) **H**	8:03 PM	(0.70) L		
4:05 AM	(0.73) L	12:12 PM	(1.62) **H**	8:05 PM	(0.62) L
5:12 AM	(0.72) L	12:49 PM	(1.70) **H**	8:25 PM	(0.55) L
6:06 AM	(0.68) L	1:26 PM	(1.76) **H**	8:49 PM	(0.51) L
6:54 AM	(0.64) L	2:00 PM	(1.80) **H**	9:15 PM	(0.48) L

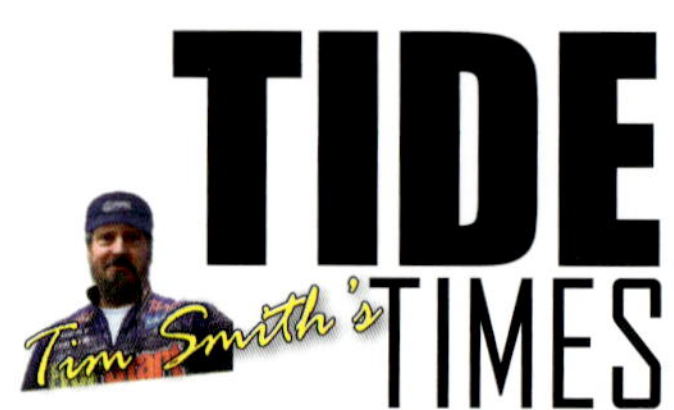

POPULAR TIDE ADJUSTMENTS

Arno Bay	+ 1hr 4min
Cape Catastrophe	- 30min
Ceduna	- 2hr 30min
Coffin Bay	+ 1hr 30min
Elliston/Cape Finnis	- 45min
Louth Bay	+ 8min
Marion Bay	+ 17min
Port Augusta	+ 6hr
Port Neill	+ 48min
Smoky Bay	- 35min
Streaky Bay	- 25min
Tumby Bay	+ 25min
Whyalla	+ 5hr
Port Victoria	+ 1hr 15min
Franklin Harbour	+ 2hr 40min
Cape Jervis	+ 2hr 5min
Wedge Island	+ 10min
Vivonne Bay	- 1hr 30min
Penneshaw	+ 1hr 20min
American River	+ 2hr 15min
Althorpe Island	+ 14min
Stenhouse Bay	+ 13min
Port Pirie	+ 5hr 30min

Port Lincoln

Day	Date	Tide 1
Wed	1	3:06 AM (0.94) **H**
Thu	2	3:30 AM (0.97) **H**
Fri	3	3:54 AM (1.00) **H**
Sat	4	4:18 AM (1.04) **H**
Sun	5	4:45 AM (1.07) **H**
Mon	6	5:15 AM (1.12) **H**
Tue	7	5:48 AM (1.16) **H**
Wed	8	6:31 AM (1.21) **H**
Thu	9	12:12 AM (0.64) L
Fri	10	10:15 AM (1.40) **H**
Sat	11	11:23 AM (1.55) **H**
Sun	12	12:22 PM (1.69) **H**
Mon	13	3:19 AM (0.77) **H**
Tue	14 ●	3:23 AM (0.77) **H**
Wed	15	3:36 AM (0.79) **H**
Thu	16	3:49 AM (0.83) **H**
Fri	17	3:59 AM (0.91) **H**
Sat	18	4:05 AM (1.02) **H**
Sun	19	4:19 AM (1.14) **H**
Mon	20	4:45 AM (1.24) **H**
Tue	21	5:18 AM (1.31) **H**
Wed	22	5:56 AM (1.32) **H**
Thu	23	6:45 AM (1.30) **H**
Fri	24	9:46 AM (1.31) **H**
Sat	25	11:11 AM (1.40) **H**
Sun	26	12:08 PM (1.49) **H**
Mon	27	2:38 AM (0.83) **H**
Tue	28	2:34 AM (0.88) **H**
Wed	29	2:45 AM (0.94) **H**
Thu	30 ○	3:02 AM (1.00) **H**
Fri	31	3:21 AM (1.07) **H**

Tide 2		Tide 3		Tide 4	
7:37 AM	(0.60) L	2:33 PM	(1.82) **H**	9:41 PM	(0.47) L
8:15 AM	(0.57) L	3:04 PM	(1.81) **H**	10:06 PM	(0.47) L
8:50 AM	(0.56) L	3:33 PM	(1.77) **H**	10:31 PM	(0.48) L
9:24 AM	(0.59) L	4:00 PM	(1.70) **H**	10:55 PM	(0.50) L
10:00 AM	(0.65) L	4:26 PM	(1.60) **H**	11:17 PM	(0.52) L
10:38 AM	(0.73) L	4:51 PM	(1.46) **H**	11:38 PM	(0.55) L
11:26 AM	(0.82) L	5:15 PM	(1.29) **H**	11:58 PM	(0.60) L
12:28 PM	(0.93) L	5:31 PM	(1.10) **H**		
8:17 AM	(1.27) **H**	11:54 PM	(0.67) L		
9:57 PM	(0.63) L				
8:50 PM	(0.50) L				
8:59 PM	(0.40) L				
4:44 AM	(0.76) L	1:15 PM	(1.79) **H**	9:23 PM	(0.36) L
5:54 AM	(0.70) L	2:02 PM	(1.85) **H**	9:46 PM	(0.37) L
7:03 AM	(0.63) L	2:40 PM	(1.85) **H**	10:03 PM	(0.43) L
8:11 AM	(0.57) L	3:08 PM	(1.79) **H**	10:15 PM	(0.49) L
8:57 AM	(0.54) L	3:29 PM	(1.69) **H**	10:25 PM	(0.52) L
9:31 AM	(0.55) L	3:45 PM	(1.58) **H**	10:31 PM	(0.53) L
10:04 AM	(0.61) L	4:04 PM	(1.46) **H**	10:38 PM	(0.50) L
10:37 AM	(0.70) L	4:22 PM	(1.34) **H**	10:47 PM	(0.47) L
11:15 AM	(0.81) L	4:36 PM	(1.21) **H**	11:01 PM	(0.46) L
11:57 AM	(0.94) L	4:12 PM	(1.09) **H**	11:14 PM	(0.49) L
12:59 PM	(1.06) L	2:14 PM	(1.07) **H**	11:07 PM	(0.54) L
10:39 PM	(0.59) L				
9:18 PM	(0.60) L				
8:37 PM	(0.55) L				
4:56 AM	(0.79) L	12:54 PM	(1.59) **H**	8:36 PM	(0.49) L
6:12 AM	(0.72) L	1:32 PM	(1.67) **H**	8:48 PM	(0.44) L
7:23 AM	(0.63) L	2:06 PM	(1.73) **H**	9:07 PM	(0.40) L
8:08 AM	(0.54) L	2:36 PM	(1.77) **H**	9:27 PM	(0.37) L
8:44 AM	(0.48) L	3:03 PM	(1.77) **H**	9:47 PM	(0.35) L

POPULAR TIDE ADJUSTMENTS

Arno Bay	+ 1hr 4min
Cape Catastrophe	- 30min
Ceduna	- 2hr 30min
Coffin Bay	+ 1hr 30min
Elliston/Cape Finnis	- 45min
Louth Bay	+ 8min
Marion Bay	+ 17min
Port Augusta	+ 6hr
Port Neill	+ 48min
Smoky Bay	- 35min
Streaky Bay	- 25min
Tumby Bay	+ 25min
Whyalla	+ 5hr
Port Victoria	+ 1hr 15min
Franklin Harbour	+ 2hr 40min
Cape Jervis	+ 2hr 5min
Wedge Island	+ 10min
Vivonne Bay	- 1hr 30min
Penneshaw	+ 1hr 20min
American River	+ 2hr 15min
Althorpe Island	+ 14min
Stenhouse Bay	+ 13min
Port Pirie	+ 5hr 30min

Port Lincoln

Day	Date	Tide 1
Sat	1	3:40 AM (1.14) **H**
Sun	2	4:00 AM (1.21) **H**
Mon	3	4:20 AM (1.27) **H**
Tue	4	4:42 AM (1.33) **H**
Wed	5	5:04 AM (1.37) **H**
Thu	6	5:31 AM (1.39) **H**
Fri	7	6:05 AM (1.36) **H**
Sat	8	9:44 AM (1.32) **H**
Sun	9	11:34 AM (1.45) **H**
Mon	10	12:50 PM (1.59) **H**
Tue	11	3:06 AM (0.83) **H**
Wed	12	3:00 AM (0.86) **H**
Thu	13 ●	3:06 AM (0.93) **H**
Fri	14	3:16 AM (1.03) **H**
Sat	15	3:26 AM (1.15) **H**
Sun	16	3:35 AM (1.28) **H**
Mon	17	3:52 AM (1.39) **H**
Tue	18	4:15 AM (1.46) **H**
Wed	19	4:40 AM (1.47) **H**
Thu	20	5:07 AM (1.43) **H**
Fri	21	5:34 AM (1.35) **H**
Sat	22	6:02 AM (1.23) **H**
Sun	23	11:14 AM (1.24) **H**
Mon	24	12:23 PM (1.36) **H**
Tue	25	2:28 AM (0.88) **H**
Wed	26	2:17 AM (0.94) **H**
Thu	27	2:24 AM (1.02) **H**
Fri	28 ○	2:37 AM (1.12) **H**
Sat	29	2:53 AM (1.22) **H**
Sun	30	3:10 AM (1.32) **H**
Mon	31	3:28 AM (1.42) **H**

Tide 2		Tide 3		Tide 4	
9:15 AM	(0.46) L	3:29 PM	(1.72) **H**	10:06 PM	(0.35) L
9:44 AM	(0.47) L	3:51 PM	(1.63) **H**	10:22 PM	(0.36) L
10:13 AM	(0.51) L	4:12 PM	(1.50) **H**	10:35 PM	(0.39) L
10:44 AM	(0.60) L	4:30 PM	(1.34) **H**	10:45 PM	(0.42) L
11:17 AM	(0.71) L	4:41 PM	(1.16) **H**	10:45 PM	(0.45) L
11:58 AM	(0.85) L	3:29 PM	(0.99) **H**	10:37 PM	(0.47) L
10:14 PM	(0.47) L				
9:21 PM	(0.42) L				
8:52 PM	(0.35) L				
8:49 PM	(0.30) L				
5:24 AM	(0.78) L	1:37 PM	(1.69) **H**	9:00 PM	(0.29) L
7:34 AM	(0.64) L	2:12 PM	(1.74) **H**	9:12 PM	(0.32) L
8:13 AM	(0.51) L	2:40 PM	(1.72) **H**	9:23 PM	(0.35) L
8:45 AM	(0.42) L	3:00 PM	(1.65) **H**	9:33 PM	(0.38) L
9:13 AM	(0.39) L	3:15 PM	(1.55) **H**	9:42 PM	(0.38) L
9:39 AM	(0.42) L	3:29 PM	(1.45) **H**	9:48 PM	(0.35) L
10:03 AM	(0.48) L	3:44 PM	(1.34) **H**	9:54 PM	(0.32) L
10:29 AM	(0.57) L	4:00 PM	(1.24) **H**	10:02 PM	(0.31) L
10:56 AM	(0.68) L	4:12 PM	(1.12) **H**	10:13 PM	(0.33) L
11:27 AM	(0.80) L	3:00 PM	(1.02) **H**	10:15 PM	(0.39) L
12:02 PM	(0.94) L	2:15 PM	(1.01) **H**	10:04 PM	(0.45) L
9:44 PM	(0.50) L				
8:37 PM	(0.50) L				
8:12 PM	(0.46) L				
5:26 AM	(0.80) L	1:01 PM	(1.47) **H**	8:13 PM	(0.40) L
7:11 AM	(0.66) L	1:31 PM	(1.57) **H**	8:23 PM	(0.35) L
7:44 AM	(0.52) L	2:00 PM	(1.64) **H**	8:39 PM	(0.30) L
8:15 AM	(0.41) L	2:26 PM	(1.66) **H**	8:57 PM	(0.27) L
8:44 AM	(0.33) L	2:50 PM	(1.64) **H**	9:15 PM	(0.25) L
9:12 AM	(0.30) L	3:13 PM	(1.56) **H**	9:29 PM	(0.26) L
9:39 AM	(0.31) L	3:33 PM	(1.44) **H**	9:40 PM	(0.28) L

POPULAR TIDE ADJUSTMENTS

Arno Bay	+ 1hr 4min
Cape Catastrophe	- 30min
Ceduna	- 2hr 30min
Coffin Bay	+ 1hr 30min
Elliston/Cape Finnis	- 45min
Louth Bay	+ 8min
Marion Bay	+ 17min
Port Augusta	+ 6hr
Port Neill	+ 48min
Smoky Bay	- 35min
Streaky Bay	- 25min
Tumby Bay	+ 25min
Whyalla	+ 5hr
Port Victoria	+ 1hr 15min
Franklin Harbour	+ 2hr 40min
Cape Jervis	+ 2hr 5min
Wedge Island	+ 10min
Vivonne Bay	- 1hr 30min
Penneshaw	+ 1hr 20min
American River	+ 2hr 15min
Althorpe Island	+ 14min
Stenhouse Bay	+ 13min
Port Pirie	+ 5hr 30min

Port Lincoln

Day	Date	Tide 1
Tue	1	3:46 AM (1.49) H
Wed	2	4:05 AM (1.53) H
Thu	3	4:26 AM (1.53) H
Fri	4	4:49 AM (1.49) H
Sat	5	5:15 AM (1.39) H
Sun	6	5:43 AM (1.23) H
Mon	7	12:17 PM (1.34) H
Tue	8	2:43 AM (0.88) H
Wed	9	2:17 AM (0.92) H
Thu	10	2:15 AM (1.01) H
Fri	11 ●	2:23 AM (1.14) H
Sat	12	2:34 AM (1.27) H
Sun	13	2:46 AM (1.40) H
Mon	14	3:00 AM (1.52) H
Tue	15	3:20 AM (1.59) H
Wed	16	3:43 AM (1.61) H
Thu	17	4:06 AM (1.57) H
Fri	18	4:29 AM (1.49) H
Sat	19	4:50 AM (1.37) H
Sun	20	5:10 AM (1.22) H
Mon	21	5:26 AM (1.07) H
Tue	22	2:38 AM (0.92) H
Wed	23	1:51 AM (0.95) H
Thu	24	1:42 AM (1.03) H
Fri	25	1:47 AM (1.15) H
Sat	26	2:00 AM (1.28) H
Sun	27 ○	2:16 AM (1.41) H
Mon	28	2:34 AM (1.53) H
Tue	29	2:53 AM (1.62) H
Wed	30	3:12 AM (1.68) H

SEPTEMBER 2026

Tide 2		Tide 3		Tide 4	
10:05 AM	(0.38) L	3:49 PM	(1.28) **H**	9:45 PM	(0.31) L
10:32 AM	(0.48) L	4:00 PM	(1.12) **H**	9:44 PM	(0.32) L
11:00 AM	(0.62) L	3:56 PM	(0.96) **H**	9:38 PM	(0.33) L
11:30 AM	(0.79) L	2:07 PM	(0.91) **H**	9:31 PM	(0.33) L
12:12 PM	(0.98) L	1:21 PM	(0.98) L	9:04 PM	(0.33) L
7:54 AM	(1.17) L	10:00 AM	(1.20) **H**	8:27 PM	(0.32) L
8:09 PM	(0.30) L				
6:53 AM	(0.83) L	1:00 PM	(1.46) **H**	8:08 PM	(0.29) L
7:18 AM	(0.64) L	1:30 PM	(1.53) **H**	8:16 PM	(0.29) L
7:45 AM	(0.47) L	1:56 PM	(1.54) **H**	8:26 PM	(0.31) L
8:10 AM	(0.36) L	2:18 PM	(1.50) **H**	8:36 PM	(0.31) L
8:36 AM	(0.29) L	2:36 PM	(1.43) **H**	8:46 PM	(0.30) L
9:01 AM	(0.27) L	2:51 PM	(1.34) **H**	8:56 PM	(0.28) L
9:26 AM	(0.30) L	3:06 PM	(1.26) **H**	9:01 PM	(0.25) L
9:48 AM	(0.36) L	3:22 PM	(1.17) **H**	9:09 PM	(0.23) L
10:12 AM	(0.44) L	3:39 PM	(1.09) **H**	9:19 PM	(0.24) L
10:36 AM	(0.55) L	3:50 PM	(0.99) **H**	9:27 PM	(0.29) L
11:03 AM	(0.68) L	2:24 PM	(0.91) **H**	9:26 PM	(0.36) L
11:32 AM	(0.82) L	1:56 PM	(0.91) **H**	9:17 PM	(0.43) L
12:15 PM	(0.96) L	1:17 PM	(0.96) L	8:41 PM	(0.48) L
7:31 AM	(1.02) L	11:09 AM	(1.10) **H**	7:42 PM	(0.47) L
6:53 AM	(0.90) L	12:12 PM	(1.23) **H**	7:29 PM	(0.42) L
6:50 AM	(0.74) L	12:44 PM	(1.33) **H**	7:32 PM	(0.36) L
7:09 AM	(0.58) L	1:12 PM	(1.42) **H**	7:44 PM	(0.31) L
7:35 AM	(0.43) L	1:39 PM	(1.46) **H**	8:00 PM	(0.27) L
8:03 AM	(0.30) L	2:06 PM	(1.46) **H**	8:16 PM	(0.25) L
8:32 AM	(0.22) L	2:31 PM	(1.40) **H**	8:31 PM	(0.25) L
9:00 AM	(0.19) L	2:54 PM	(1.29) **H**	8:43 PM	(0.26) L
9:28 AM	(0.22) L	3:13 PM	(1.15) **H**	8:47 PM	(0.27) L
9:55 AM	(0.30) L	3:25 PM	(1.00) **H**	8:46 PM	(0.27) L

POPULAR TIDE ADJUSTMENTS

Arno Bay	+ 1hr 4min
Cape Catastrophe	- 30min
Ceduna	- 2hr 30min
Coffin Bay	+ 1hr 30min
Elliston/Cape Finnis	- 45min
Louth Bay	+ 8min
Marion Bay	+ 17min
Port Augusta	+ 6hr
Port Neill	+ 48min
Smoky Bay	- 35min
Streaky Bay	- 25min
Tumby Bay	+ 25min
Whyalla	+ 5hr
Port Victoria	+ 1hr 15min
Franklin Harbour	+ 2hr 40min
Cape Jervis	+ 2hr 5min
Wedge Island	+ 10min
Vivonne Bay	- 1hr 30min
Penneshaw	+ 1hr 20min
American River	+ 2hr 15min
Althorpe Island	+ 14min
Stenhouse Bay	+ 13min
Port Pirie	+ 5hr 30min

Port Lincoln

Day	Date		Tide 1
Thu	1		3:32 AM (1.68) H
Fri	2		3:54 AM (1.62) H
Sat	3		4:18 AM (1.51) H
Sun	4		5:43 AM (1.34) H
Mon	5		6:00 AM (1.14) H
Tue	6		5:37 AM (0.94) H
Wed	7		2:41 AM (0.95) H
Thu	8		2:24 AM (1.06) H
Fri	9		2:28 AM (1.20) H
Sat	10		2:38 AM (1.35) H
Sun	11	●	2:52 AM (1.49) H
Mon	12		3:08 AM (1.61) H
Tue	13		3:29 AM (1.69) H
Wed	14		3:50 AM (1.71) H
Thu	15		4:14 AM (1.69) H
Fri	16		4:37 AM (1.62) H
Sat	17		5:00 AM (1.51) H
Sun	18		5:22 AM (1.38) H
Mon	19		5:41 AM (1.23) H
Tue	20		5:54 AM (1.07) H
Wed	21		2:58 AM (0.95) H
Thu	22		2:04 AM (1.01) H
Fri	23		1:56 AM (1.13) H
Sat	24		2:04 AM (1.29) H
Sun	25		2:19 AM (1.45) H
Mon	26	○	2:38 AM (1.60) H
Tue	27		3:00 AM (1.71) H
Wed	28		3:22 AM (1.78) H
Thu	29		3:45 AM (1.79) H
Fri	30		4:10 AM (1.74) H
Sat	31		4:35 AM (1.63) H

OCTOBER 2026

Tide 2		Tide 3		Tide 4	
10:22 AM	(0.44) L	3:28 PM	(0.86) **H**	8:44 PM	(0.27) L
10:48 AM	(0.60) L	1:49 PM	(0.79) **H**	8:45 PM	(0.27) L
11:15 AM	(0.77) L	1:20 PM	(0.84) **H**	8:35 PM	(0.29) L
12:53 PM	(0.94) L	1:41 PM	(0.94) L	9:00 PM	(0.32) L
8:38 AM	(1.05) L	11:36 AM	(1.09) **H**	8:33 PM	(0.35) L
7:51 AM	(0.90) L	1:08 PM	(1.20) **H**	8:15 PM	(0.37) L
7:50 AM	(0.70) L	1:39 PM	(1.26) **H**	8:16 PM	(0.37) L
8:09 AM	(0.53) L	2:05 PM	(1.28) **H**	8:24 PM	(0.36) L
8:32 AM	(0.39) L	2:30 PM	(1.26) **H**	8:33 PM	(0.35) L
8:56 AM	(0.29) L	2:50 PM	(1.22) **H**	8:45 PM	(0.32) L
9:21 AM	(0.23) L	3:10 PM	(1.17) **H**	8:56 PM	(0.29) L
9:46 AM	(0.22) L	3:28 PM	(1.11) **H**	9:06 PM	(0.26) L
10:11 AM	(0.24) L	3:46 PM	(1.06) **H**	9:16 PM	(0.24) L
10:34 AM	(0.29) L	4:06 PM	(1.00) **H**	9:29 PM	(0.24) L
10:58 AM	(0.37) L	4:24 PM	(0.93) **H**	9:42 PM	(0.27) L
11:22 AM	(0.47) L	4:37 PM	(0.86) **H**	9:51 PM	(0.33) L
11:49 AM	(0.59) L	3:18 PM	(0.79) **H**	9:53 PM	(0.40) L
12:21 PM	(0.71) L	2:45 PM	(0.79) **H**	9:45 PM	(0.47) L
8:38 PM	(0.53) L				
7:43 PM	(0.51) L				
7:44 AM	(0.89) L	12:23 PM	(1.06) **H**	7:32 PM	(0.46) L
7:33 AM	(0.72) L	1:08 PM	(1.14) **H**	7:40 PM	(0.41) L
7:53 AM	(0.55) L	1:43 PM	(1.20) **H**	7:54 PM	(0.37) L
8:20 AM	(0.39) L	2:15 PM	(1.21) **H**	8:11 PM	(0.35) L
8:50 AM	(0.25) L	2:46 PM	(1.18) **H**	8:27 PM	(0.34) L
9:21 AM	(0.17) L	3:15 PM	(1.10) **H**	8:38 PM	(0.33) L
9:52 AM	(0.15) L	3:40 PM	(0.98) **H**	8:45 PM	(0.32) L
10:22 AM	(0.20) L	3:58 PM	(0.85) **H**	8:51 PM	(0.30) L
10:52 AM	(0.31) L	4:06 PM	(0.73) **H**	8:56 PM	(0.28) L
11:22 AM	(0.45) L	4:03 PM	(0.66) **H**	9:02 PM	(0.28) L
11:51 AM	(0.60) L	2:02 PM	(0.67) **H**	9:08 PM	(0.30) L

POPULAR TIDE ADJUSTMENTS

Arno Bay	+ 1hr 4min
Cape Catastrophe	- 30min
Ceduna	- 2hr 30min
Coffin Bay	+ 1hr 30min
Elliston/Cape Finnis	- 45min
Louth Bay	+ 8min
Marion Bay	+ 17min
Port Augusta	+ 6hr
Port Neill	+ 48min
Smoky Bay	- 35min
Streaky Bay	- 25min
Tumby Bay	+ 25min
Whyalla	+ 5hr
Port Victoria	+ 1hr 15min
Franklin Harbour	+ 2hr 40min
Cape Jervis	+ 2hr 5min
Wedge Island	+ 10min
Vivonne Bay	- 1hr 30min
Penneshaw	+ 1hr 20min
American River	+ 2hr 15min
Althorpe Island	+ 14min
Stenhouse Bay	+ 13min
Port Pirie	+ 5hr 30min

Port Lincoln

Day	Date		Tide 1
Sun	1		5:00 AM (1.47) H
Mon	2		5:25 AM (1.27) H
Tue	3		5:36 AM (1.07) H
Wed	4		2:41 AM (0.94) H
Thu	5		1:39 AM (1.03) H
Fri	6		1:31 AM (1.19) H
Sat	7		1:40 AM (1.35) H
Sun	8		1:56 AM (1.51) H
Mon	9	●	2:15 AM (1.63) H
Tue	10		2:38 AM (1.71) H
Wed	11		3:03 AM (1.75) H
Thu	12		3:29 AM (1.75) H
Fri	13		3:55 AM (1.71) H
Sat	14		4:21 AM (1.63) H
Sun	15		4:45 AM (1.53) H
Mon	16		5:11 AM (1.40) H
Tue	17		5:34 AM (1.26) H
Wed	18		5:55 AM (1.11) H
Thu	19		5:36 AM (0.94) H
Fri	20		1:03 AM (1.04) H
Sat	21		1:01 AM (1.20) H
Sun	22		1:17 AM (1.38) H
Mon	23		1:40 AM (1.56) H
Tue	24		2:06 AM (1.70) H
Wed	25	○	2:35 AM (1.80) H
Thu	26		3:04 AM (1.84) H
Fri	27		3:34 AM (1.81) H
Sat	28		4:03 AM (1.72) H
Sun	29		4:31 AM (1.58) H
Mon	30		5:00 AM (1.42) H

NOVEMBER 2026

Tide 2		Tide 3		Tide 4	
12:25 PM	(0.74) L	1:45 PM	(0.75) **H**	8:56 PM	(0.37) L
8:16 PM	(0.45) L				
7:29 PM	(0.51) L				
7:47 AM	(0.84) L	12:21 PM	(0.97) **H**	7:07 PM	(0.52) L
7:41 AM	(0.67) L	1:05 PM	(0.97) **H**	7:10 PM	(0.51) L
8:00 AM	(0.52) L	1:35 PM	(0.97) **H**	7:14 PM	(0.48) L
8:21 AM	(0.41) L	2:02 PM	(0.96) **H**	7:24 PM	(0.44) L
8:45 AM	(0.32) L	2:27 PM	(0.94) **H**	7:42 PM	(0.39) L
9:09 AM	(0.26) L	2:51 PM	(0.93) **H**	8:01 PM	(0.35) L
9:34 AM	(0.23) L	3:15 PM	(0.91) **H**	8:21 PM	(0.32) L
10:00 AM	(0.24) L	3:38 PM	(0.89) **H**	8:41 PM	(0.31) L
10:26 AM	(0.28) L	4:00 PM	(0.87) **H**	9:01 PM	(0.32) L
10:51 AM	(0.34) L	4:22 PM	(0.83) **H**	9:20 PM	(0.34) L
11:18 AM	(0.42) L	4:44 PM	(0.79) **H**	9:36 PM	(0.40) L
11:48 AM	(0.50) L	5:04 PM	(0.75) **H**	9:46 PM	(0.47) L
12:25 PM	(0.58) L	5:28 PM	(0.70) **H**	9:49 PM	(0.56) L
1:21 PM	(0.65) L	3:10 PM	(0.66) **H**	4:53 PM	(0.65) L
5:31 PM	(0.61) L				
5:53 PM	(0.57) L				
7:13 AM	(0.76) L	12:10 PM	(0.91) **H**	6:15 PM	(0.54) L
7:38 AM	(0.57) L	1:15 PM	(0.92) **H**	6:37 PM	(0.51) L
8:11 AM	(0.39) L	2:01 PM	(0.92) **H**	6:59 PM	(0.49) L
8:45 AM	(0.26) L	2:42 PM	(0.88) **H**	7:18 PM	(0.47) L
9:21 AM	(0.18) L	3:18 PM	(0.81) **H**	7:37 PM	(0.43) L
9:57 AM	(0.17) L	3:49 PM	(0.72) **H**	7:56 PM	(0.40) L
10:32 AM	(0.22) L	4:15 PM	(0.64) **H**	8:14 PM	(0.36) L
11:07 AM	(0.31) L	4:25 PM	(0.58) **H**	8:32 PM	(0.34) L
11:40 AM	(0.43) L	4:25 PM	(0.57) **H**	8:52 PM	(0.36) L
12:09 PM	(0.54) L	4:35 PM	(0.60) **H**	9:13 PM	(0.42) L
12:32 PM	(0.62) L	5:06 PM	(0.65) **H**	9:28 PM	(0.52) L

Port Lincoln

POPULAR TIDE ADJUSTMENTS

Arno Bay	+ 1hr 4min
Cape Catastrophe	- 30min
Ceduna	- 2hr 30min
Coffin Bay	+ 1hr 30min
Elliston/Cape Finnis	- 45min
Louth Bay	+ 8min
Marion Bay	+ 17min
Port Augusta	+ 6hr
Port Neill	+ 48min
Smoky Bay	- 35min
Streaky Bay	- 25min
Tumby Bay	+ 25min
Whyalla	+ 5hr
Port Victoria	+ 1hr 15min
Franklin Harbour	+ 2hr 40min
Cape Jervis	+ 2hr 5min
Wedge Island	+ 10min
Vivonne Bay	- 1hr 30min
Penneshaw	+ 1hr 20min
American River	+ 2hr 15min
Althorpe Island	+ 14min
Stenhouse Bay	+ 13min
Port Pirie	+ 5hr 30min

Day	Date	Tide 1
Tue	1	5:25 AM (1.24) **H**
Wed	2	5:38 AM (1.06) **H**
Thu	3	3:45 AM (0.92) **H**
Fri	4	12:24 AM (1.07) **H**
Sat	5	12:36 AM (1.25) **H**
Sun	6	12:57 AM (1.40) **H**
Mon	7	1:21 AM (1.53) **H**
Tue	8	1:50 AM (1.63) **H**
Wed	9 ●	2:20 AM (1.69) **H**
Thu	10	2:51 AM (1.72) **H**
Fri	11	3:21 AM (1.72) **H**
Sat	12	3:51 AM (1.69) **H**
Sun	13	4:19 AM (1.63) **H**
Mon	14	4:46 AM (1.55) **H**
Tue	15	5:14 AM (1.44) **H**
Wed	16	5:39 AM (1.31) **H**
Thu	17	6:03 AM (1.16) **H**
Fri	18	1:11 AM (0.84) L
Sat	19	2:45 PM (0.59) L
Sun	20	8:08 AM (0.59) L
Mon	21	12:32 AM (1.39) **H**
Tue	22	1:12 AM (1.56) **H**
Wed	23	1:53 AM (1.69) **H**
Thu	24 ○	2:33 AM (1.77) **H**
Fri	25	3:12 AM (1.79) **H**
Sat	26	3:47 AM (1.76) **H**
Sun	27	4:16 AM (1.66) **H**
Mon	28	4:41 AM (1.53) **H**
Tue	29	5:02 AM (1.38) **H**
Wed	30	5:22 AM (1.23) **H**
Thu	31	5:34 AM (1.08) **H**

Tide 2		Tide 3		Tide 4	
12:53 PM	(0.65) L	6:18 PM	(0.70) **H**	9:13 PM	(0.67) L
1:22 PM	(0.65) L				
2:32 PM	(0.64) L				
4:13 PM	(0.60) L				
8:17 AM	(0.58) L	1:16 PM	(0.67) **H**	5:06 PM	(0.56) L
8:30 AM	(0.47) L	1:56 PM	(0.70) **H**	5:54 PM	(0.52) L
8:47 AM	(0.38) L	2:28 PM	(0.73) **H**	6:38 PM	(0.49) L
9:10 AM	(0.31) L	2:57 PM	(0.76) **H**	7:18 PM	(0.45) L
9:35 AM	(0.27) L	3:24 PM	(0.79) **H**	7:55 PM	(0.42) L
10:01 AM	(0.26) L	3:49 PM	(0.81) **H**	8:28 PM	(0.40) L
10:29 AM	(0.27) L	4:15 PM	(0.82) **H**	8:58 PM	(0.39) L
10:55 AM	(0.30) L	4:39 PM	(0.83) **H**	9:26 PM	(0.40) L
11:22 AM	(0.33) L	5:05 PM	(0.83) **H**	9:53 PM	(0.44) L
11:49 AM	(0.37) L	5:34 PM	(0.84) **H**	10:18 PM	(0.51) L
12:16 PM	(0.41) L	6:10 PM	(0.84) **H**	10:46 PM	(0.60) L
12:45 PM	(0.45) L	6:56 PM	(0.86) **H**	11:27 PM	(0.72) L
1:16 PM	(0.50) L	8:18 PM	(0.91) **H**		
6:23 AM	(0.99) **H**	1:53 PM	(0.55) L	11:00 PM	(1.04) **H**
11:52 PM	(1.21) **H**				
1:34 PM	(0.65) **H**	4:12 PM	(0.62) L		
8:32 AM	(0.40) L	2:38 PM	(0.67) **H**	5:22 PM	(0.61) L
9:08 AM	(0.26) L	3:20 PM	(0.68) **H**	6:13 PM	(0.58) L
9:45 AM	(0.17) L	3:55 PM	(0.66) **H**	6:57 PM	(0.53) L
10:22 AM	(0.15) L	4:24 PM	(0.64) **H**	7:39 PM	(0.47) L
10:55 AM	(0.18) L	4:48 PM	(0.63) **H**	8:20 PM	(0.43) L
11:21 AM	(0.26) L	5:06 PM	(0.64) **H**	9:00 PM	(0.41) L
11:40 AM	(0.34) L	5:15 PM	(0.70) **H**	9:39 PM	(0.42) L
11:52 AM	(0.41) L	5:23 PM	(0.79) **H**	10:20 PM	(0.48) L
12:00 PM	(0.43) L	5:47 PM	(0.90) **H**	11:06 PM	(0.58) L
12:05 PM	(0.42) L	6:24 PM	(0.99) **H**	11:58 PM	(0.71) L
12:15 PM	(0.39) L	7:15 PM	(1.05) **H**		

POPULAR RIGS

Saltwater Rigs

Surface Float Rig

An excellent surface salmon rig consists of a styrene float, a couple of 4/0 hooks and a small sinker for weight. The hooks are tied on a metre or so of 15 kg monofilament trace and are spaced to hold a full pilchard comfortably. Slip a running ball sinker down the trace right on to the top hook. Then slip on a running styrene float and attach the top of the trace to a good quality swivel. This will allow the float to suspend your bait at the correct depth for feeding salmon. Should you require the bait to be set deeper, simply extend the trace length.

This rig casts reasonably well from a threadline or sidecast outfit and can be modified easily to suit small or large salmon, tommy ruff, tailor (with the inclusion of a light wire trace) and trevally.

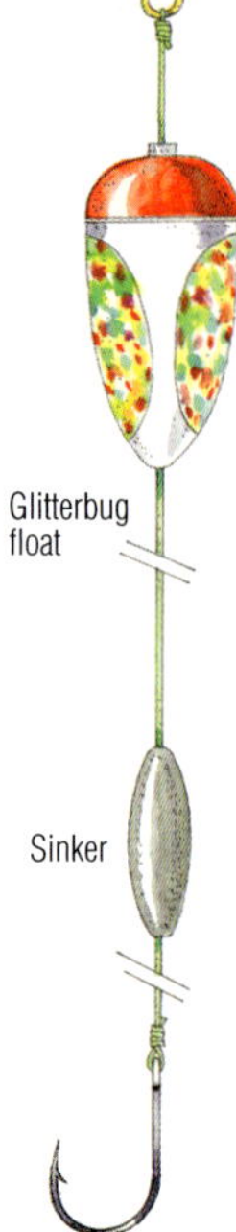

3–6 kg fluorocarbon leader to bait

5 kg mono

Freshwater Rig

Standard Paternoster for Boat and Bank

This is a standard rig for many Australian native species from barra to cod, using anything from a worm, to a yabby, to a live bait or prawn for barra.

You can vary the length of the droppers, depending on conditions, and the 3-way swivel could be substituted with a brass ring if the fish encountered are likely to pull your arms off! Add a red bead too—it can add a touch of spark and get those fish biting.

Fixed teardrop sinker

POPULAR KNOTS

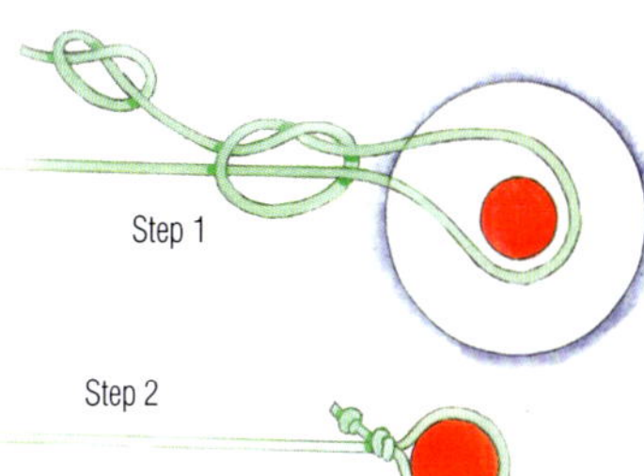

Arbor Knot

This is a very fast and secure knot for attaching line to the reel. Pass the tag end of the line around the spool and form an overhand knot with the tag end around the main line. Then another overhand knot on the tag end of the line. Lubricate the knots if using monofilament, tighten down by pulling the main line, and trim the tag.

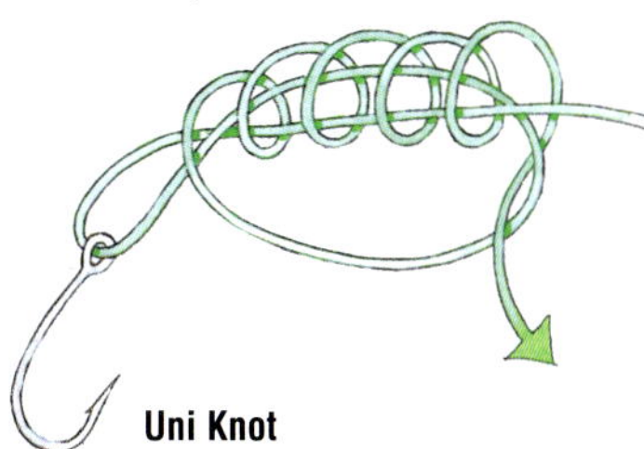

Uni Knot

An easy-to-tie versatile knot. Thread the eye of the hook with the line so the hook is suspended on a loop. Encircle the main line with the tag so another loop is formed. Wrap the double strand inside the loop with the tag. Make four wraps in all, leaving the tag protruding from the loop. Close the knot but do not pull it tight just yet. Slide the knot down onto the eye of the hook, pull it tight and trim the tag.

Homer Rhode Knot

This knot should never be used on lighter weight monofilaments, as it breaks at around 50 per cent of the line test.

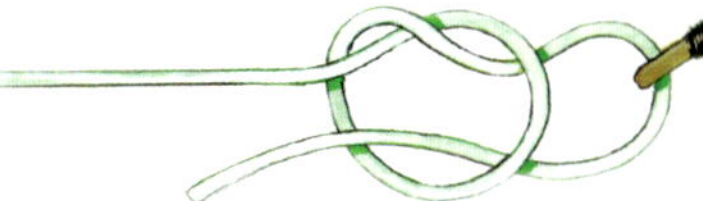

1. Form an overhand knot in the main line leaving approximately 20 cm (8 inches) of monofilament between the knot and the tag end. Pass the tag end through the hook eye and then back through the overhand knot from the same side as it exited. Tighten the overhand knot lightly to the hook eye by pulling on the tail of the hook and on the tag end of the line, while keeping the two lines parallel to prevent the hook from twisting on the knot.

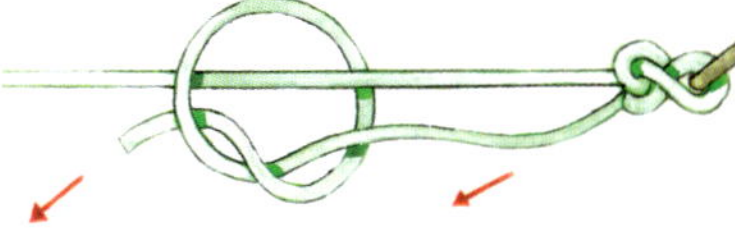

2. Make another overhand knot over the standing part of the line. This knot is the stopper for the loop, so its position determines the size of the loop, generally this knot would be 2–3 cm (1 inch) from the hook eye. Tighten this second knot and then pull on the bend of the hook and the main line at the same time.

3. The knot at the hook eye should slide up the line snugly into the second knot. Trim the tag.

FISH ID SA

BREAM
Grows to 3.5kg/60cm
GREENBACK FLOUNDER
Grows to 0.6kg
EASTERN BLUE SPOT FLATHEAD
Grows to 8kg/100cm
KING GEORGE WHITING
Grows to 2kg/67cm
MULLET
Grows to 1kg/41cm
SOUTHERN SEA GARFISH
Grows to 50cm
AUSTRALIAN SALMON
Grows to 9kg/90cm
YELLOW-EYE MULLET
Grows to 50cm/1kg
SNAPPER
Grows to 125cm/19kg
AUSTRALIAN HERRING
Grows to 40cm
SOUTHERN BLUE MORWONG
Grows to 100cm
MULLOWAY
Grows to 180cm/60kg
BLUE GROPER
Grows to 40kg/160cm
CHINAMAN LEATHERJACKET
Grows to 3.5kg/70cm

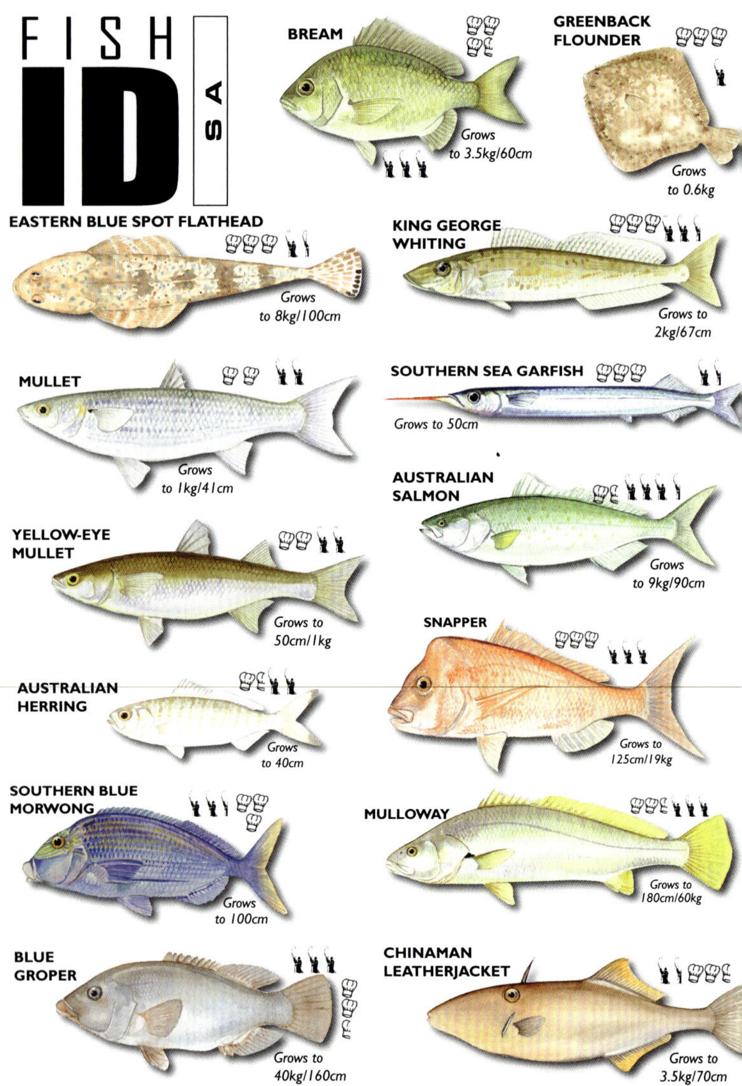

SNOOK
Grows to 5kg/110cm
SILVER TREVALLY
Grows to 11kg/100cm
LONGFIN PIKE
Grows to 2kg/90cm
SIX SPINED LEATHERJACKET,
Grows to 60cm
BASTARD TRUMPETER
Grows to 4kg/65cm
SLIMY MACKEREL
No size limit
Grows to 65cm/2kg
YELLOWTAIL SCAD
Grows to 33cm
SWEEP
Grows to 45cm/3kg
RED SNAPPER
Grows to 45cm
BLUETHROAT WRASSE
BROWN TROUT
Grows to 100cm/14kg
RAINBOW TROUT
Grows to 80cm/7kg
GRUNTER/ SILVER PERCH
Grows to 60cm/8kg
MURRAY COD
Grows to 113kg/180cm

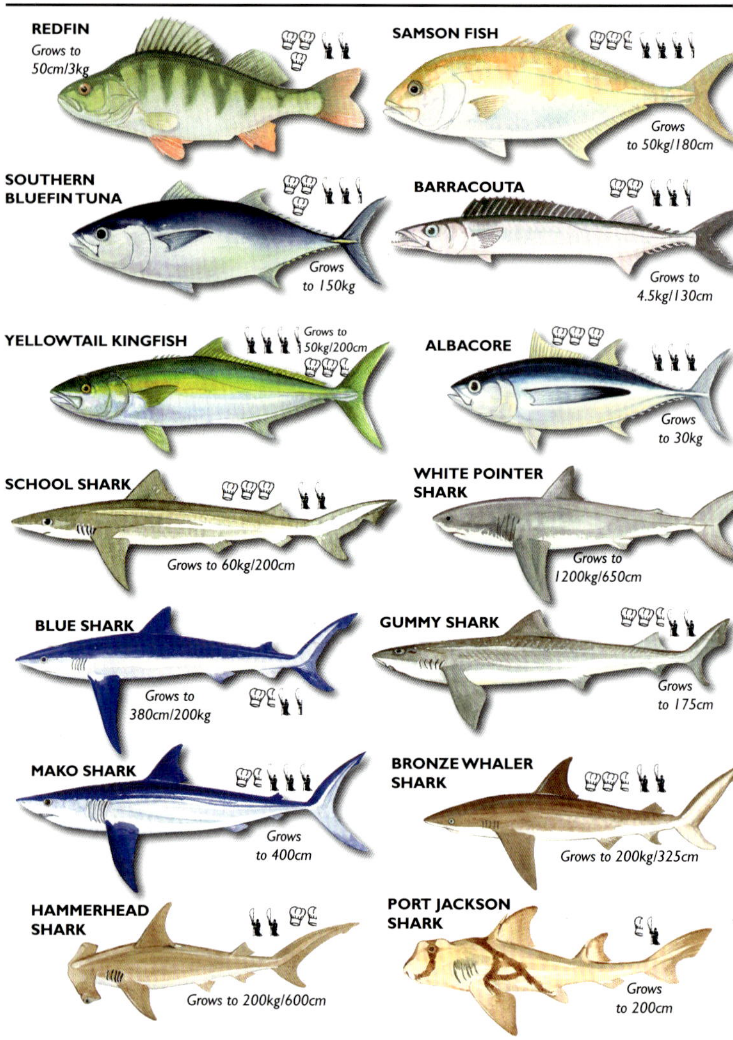
REDFIN
Grows to
50cm/3kg
SAMSON FISH
Grows
to 50kg/180cm
SOUTHERN
BLUEFIN TUNA
Grows
to 150kg
BARRACOUTA
Grows to
4.5kg/130cm
YELLOWTAIL KINGFISH
Grows to
50kg/200cm
ALBACORE
Grows
to 30kg
SCHOOL SHARK
Grows to 60kg/200cm
WHITE POINTER
SHARK
Grows to
1200kg/650cm
BLUE SHARK
Grows to
380cm/200kg
GUMMY SHARK
Grows
to 175cm
MAKO SHARK
Grows
to 400cm
BRONZE WHALER
SHARK
Grows to 200kg/325cm
HAMMERHEAD
SHARK
Grows to 200kg/600cm
PORT JACKSON
SHARK
Grows
to 200cm